J

The One Who Sees Me Lives

You who seek God,
your hearts shall live.
(Psalm 69:32)

ISBN: 978-1541108141

All Bible quotations are taken from King James Version, unless otherwise noted. Cover Design and layout – My Zion Productions.

Prologue

When Isaac was old, and his eyes were dim…
(Genesis 27:1)

Anna dabs at her eyes with a handkerchief and carefully draws the magnifying glass resting by the Bible on the table over to herself. "For some reason, people don't appreciate what they have when they have it, and don't read God's Word when they are able. Only when you lose something do you realize what you have lost. My eyesight has gotten so poor lately…."

I am sitting across from her, and with every cell of my being, I am sensing that God is speaking to me about something that I need to - am compelled, simply must - understand. Which biblical character had poor vision in the decline of life? Ah yes, of course: It was Isaac. The Scriptures describe him by stating that *his eyes were dim….* But what? What's behind this? What exactly does the Lord want to show me?

The three of us are sitting in Anna's tiny room in Ma'ale Adumim - a modern suburb of Jerusalem situated eastward of that ancient city - which I once again find surprisingly clean and cozy. We have come here to stand before God together with Anna, to seek a blessing on the book about her life that He is revealing to us and leading us toward.

The three of us are sitting in this tiny room…. It would be very fitting at this point to say something about the room's thriving plants, or about the window thrown open to the gardens – and yet, I'm not going to write about that. First of all, it doesn't really correspond to Israeli reality: Ma'ale Adumim is encircled by the desert, though the small city itself is surprisingly lush and green. But that's not really the reason, either. Here, in this room, there is simply no outside world. It is a world of its own: the world of His Word, the world of her recollections, the world of their love. *Who is this coming up from the wilderness, leaning upon her beloved?*[1] To reach Ma'ale Adumim, you actually do have to come up out of the desert, so it turns out that the spiritual geography of Anna's life is also encapsulated within these outward circumstances. Perhaps here, in the Judean Wilderness, the meaning of these words can be grasped with particular clarity: You can't go through a desert alone – you will simply not survive it if you don't rely on Him. Anna emerged out of that desert, out of that *valley of the shadow of death*[2] through which she traversed, *leaning upon her beloved* – and since then, she has always leaned upon Him. Always. Even today, when seeing her constrained mobility, one still gets the sense that she is leaning on Someone. On an Invisible Someone – on her Beloved.

The three of us begin to pray, and while praying, a verse once read in some midrash surfaces distinctly in my memory: *Why did his eyes grown dim? From the tears shed on Mount Moriah….*

Suddenly, everything falls into place. It all harmonizes into a single picture, as always occurs with one of God's puzzles. Isaac *was led as a lamb to the slaughter, and as a sheep before its shearers is silent*[3] – before the knife that was already raised above him. Anna, who as a 16-year-old girl was led out to be shot, was also delivered by God at the very last moment – with the knife already raised. This knife raised in midair and stopped by the Lord at the last moment for them both – for both Isaac and Anna – was what pierced hearts with His love. The long life that they both then lived was spent with Him, under the wings of His mercy and His blessing. And only in old age did the eyes of both – Isaac and Anna – grow *dim* from those tears that were shed under the raised knife.

So this was how it was revealed to me, and I left Anna that day grateful to God and overflowing with this new revelation. But when, upon reaching home, I searched for the place in the midrash that discusses Isaac's blindness and through which the Lord had linked Anna to Isaac for me, I was simply dumbfounded: It turns out that it was by no means the tears of Isaac himself that had caused his eyes to dim in his old age. It was the angelic tears – or God's tears, one might say – over Isaac lying on the altar that had left *"markings on his eyes." "Rabbi Eleazar Ben-Azariah said: Seeing Isaac lying on the altar, the angels wept, and the angelic tears fell on Isaac's eyes, leaving markings on his eyes. This caused Isaac's eyes to grown dim in his old age."* Yes, it's quite possible that Isaac himself also wept on the altar, but it was important for the Lord to show that He Himself is the One Who wept, and Who weeps. It was important for Him to show **His Own tears**. It's because of these divine tears shed over Isaac that his *eyes were dim* when he *was old* – and because of these divine tears shed over Anna that her eyes also grew dim in her old age.

Those who have read my book about the sufferings of Israel (*If You Be the Son of God, Come Down From the Cross*, New Wine Press, 2006), will undoubtedly understand why I was so excited, and will surely sense the connection between that book and these pages just revealed by the Lord. For those who have not read it, I would like to comment briefly. *If You Be the Son of God, Come Down From the Cross* is a book about God's love for Israel and about the invisible world of God's tears shed over Israel's suffering, with the *Aqedah*, the sacrifice of Isaac, revealed in that book as an image of Israel's ascent to the altar, the image of the beloved son who becomes a sacrificial lamb while walking down the path where his father is leading him. And specifically for that reason, I was so stunned by these divine tears over Isaac lying on the altar, shown to me in connection with Anna's story. The world does not see God's love for Israel. When addressing the chosen people's constant suffering, the world tells them: You see? God isn't saving you from your sorrows, which means He has stopped loving you and has left you. If you want to prove that He still loves you, stop suffering. *If you be the Son of God, come down from the cross.*[4] **But the Lord showed me His tears**

over Israel that are invisible to the world – and someone who has seen these tears even once can never again doubt His love for His people. Many years ago, it was Anna who asked me the question that is so frequently asked of believers: "Why was God silent during the Holocaust? Why was He silent? How could He have allowed all of that? All the atrocious suffering of millions of perfectly innocent people?" The book He gave me became His answer to me: The Lord was silent and allowed the Holocaust – He is silent and has allowed centuries of Israel's suffering – just the way He was silent over Golgotha and allowed the crucifixion: with a heart breaking from pain and with tears held back.

In this sense, the Lord is not only uniting this new story, which I am embarking on with prayer and trembling, to everything He already told me and showed me about both suffering and Israel, but He is giving me this book as if as a confirmation of the first two. On the way home that day, my husband Victor said: "Anna is an amazing embodiment of both your first book – about Job, a person who having lost all, gained God – and your second one, about the *Aqedah* and Isaac as a symbol of Israel's ascent to the altar and about the invisible, but yet real world of God's tears over Isaac's suffering." In the opening of the second book, I wrote about how it was with such heavy responsibility and fear that I shifted my focus from the suffering of a biblical personage, Job, to the suffering of my people. In some sense, this holds even more true as I shift my focus from the suffering of people generally to the suffering of one specific living (and beloved) individual from among this people. And therefore, I am approaching this book *in fear and trembling*, and with prayer and trust in God's help. Not just – and we all agree on this – to describe the heroic exploits of Anna or her rescuer, not to describe her difficult life or her walk with God. But first and foremost to glorify the Lord, Who not only by the greatness of His power preserves *those who are appointed to die*[5], but also has made the hearts of those who seek God to live.[6] And secondly, so that all that He showed us about His love for Israel in my previous book can take on flesh and blood in this story of a very corporeal *daughter of Zion*. We pray and believe that this book will become a testimony to His love; we pray that those who have not yet come to know the love of God would be drawn up into it through these pages, and that those who have already met Him and have experienced His love in their lives would be dazzled by His love and faithfulness to His people. We pray that for both believers and nonbelievers, these pages would become evidence and a testimony of how *neither death nor life, nor angels, nor principalities, nor powers, nor things present, nor things to come, nor height, nor depth, nor any other created thing, shall be able to separate us from the love of God which is in Messiah Yeshua our Lord.*[7]

Chapter 1

THE BEGINNING

But You are He who took
Me out of the womb;
You made Me trust while on
My mother's breasts.
I was cast upon You from birth.
From My mother's womb
You have been My God.
(Psalm 22:9-10)

"I'm 12 years old. I'm afraid of death, and I'm afraid of funerals. Life is so beautiful – why does it suddenly come to an end?"

Those who have never been to Ukraine cannot even imagine its lavish, profuse, bourgeoning and blossoming springtime. Of course, it wasn't always May or June, and the city sprawling across both shores of the Sluch River didn't always effloresce with the cherry-colored white and pink foam of flowering gardens, nor were the evenings always this incredible, the air thick and drunk from the scent of blooms, the black nights illuminated by myriads of stars – only in the south is there such a black sky in Ukraine, so warm and simultaneously filled with stars. No, it wasn't always summer – but that is how she remembers her childhood: These endless, carefree summer days on the Sluch, these wondrous evenings, when one is surrounded by such beauty and delight that it simply hurts – hurts from this inconceivable splendor, from this tranquility, from this blossoming. Surprising, is it not? At the end of the 1930s, the Soviet Union was far from being the most calm, idyllic place on earth. But Buzya's life, the life of a girl growing up in the midst of love, beauty, and wisdom, a life filled with peace and happiness, would have been perfectly whole were it not for the alarming tread of heavy footfalls, reverberating from somewhere beyond the as-of-yet invisible corner. What did this life hold for her? What had fate prepared for her?

And once again, as if listening to something far off that others cannot see or hear, Buzya shudders. "Life is so beautiful – why does it suddenly come to an end? Are we really all going to die? Then what is it all for?" Buzya asks her friend Nina.

"Death is still far off. Why are you already thinking about it now?" asks her friend.

But Buzya cannot think about anything else. She thinks about it all the time. She asks her parents about it. Then, her mama tells her: See, Enoch was righteous before the Lord, and he didn't die. He was taken alive into heaven: *And Enoch walked with God; and he was not, for God took him.*[8]

Buzya is staggered. Apparently, there is a way out: You don't have to die; you can go to heaven.

You can be righteous, love God, and do good deeds, and then you won't die. Then God Himself will take you to heaven. From that day on, Buzya stopped fearing death; now she had hope. And from that day on, she tried to do only good deeds and help everyone – so as to go to heaven.

***

In all likelihood, not very many of my readers remember pre-war Ukraine with its small Jewish townships and shtetls. Our story begins in one such shtetl, in the city of Lyubar in the Zhitomir Oblast. In geographic terms, Lyubar still exists today – to this day, you can easily find its name on the map of Zhitomir Oblast. But now, it's a completely different Lyubar: Only the name of the pre-war shtetl remains – along with a mass grave in a young pine forest, which grew over the site of the atrocious mass shooting in the Peschanoye district. Until recently, the small memorial set up at the site of the shooting held only a general inscription to "the victims of Fascism," without the slightest hint of the ethnicity of these "victims." Only in the 1990s did a six-pointed star appear on this memorial, attesting to the fact that the victims buried here were Jews.[9]

This town that no longer exists was completely Jewish. According to the census, of its 12,000 residents, there were no fewer than 7,000 Jews (today, you're unlikely to find even 7 Jews in the city). The first Jews had appeared here several centuries earlier: Displaced persons and refugees escaping persecution elsewhere in Europe settled in Ukraine, in its quaint villages overflowing with the bounty of the generous, fertile Ukrainian soil. Lyubar was no exception: The blue ribbon of the Sluch River, a tributary of the Dnieper River, wound its way through the city, whose numerous one-story houses and the rare two-story house were spread along the banks of the Sluch, overgrown with thick grass, weeping willows, and tall rushes. Despite its small size, Lyubar was very bustling town, and it was a happy and carefree place to live – at least, so it remains in the memory of those who grew up there. Along both sides of the river, a two-meter-wide sidewalk of planks was laid – a boardwalk. The center of town was always lit. Pre-war Lyubar was charming and picturesque – and for the Jews who lived there, it seemed that this corner in the "Pale of Settlement," this nook of beauty and fertility, had been given to them and to their children forever.

It was in this lovely, cozy Jewish shtetl, in a large two-story wooden home on the bank of the Sluch River, that the girl Buzya was born in 1925 to the young family of Eizik and Reizl Schmieger. The house belonged to her maternal grandfather, Chaim Rabinovich, and his wife Ita, who had settled in this home after the Bolshevik Revolution. The birth of Buzya, their first granddaughter, had made them grandparents. Prior to the revolution, Chaim Rabinovich kept a tavern and, in addition, an entire farm: a field, a garden, even several cows. They milked the cows, and the milk was taken to sell in the center of Lyubar. "If Sholem Aleichem had lived in prerevolutionary Lyubar," says Dmitry-Fishl, Buzya's brother (this is the first, but far from the last time we will hear him speak from these pages), "he might have written 'milkman Chaim' instead of "milkman Tevye.'" Of course, the children also helped with the farm, with most of the work, naturally, entrusted to the eldest daughter Reizl – the future mother of Buzya and Fishl. After the revolution, grandfather Chaim borrowed money from friends and bought the two-story home in the very center of Lyubar. On the lower floor of the house, he set up a business: For Pesach, he baked matzo there, and the rest of the time he produced wine, which he also sold at his shop. (To do this, he rented fields, collected the harvest, and made wine.) Grandfather Chaim rented one of the upper-story rooms out as a city library, and all the rest of the rooms were occupied by the large, tight-knit Rabinovich family. Chaim and Ita had four children: Reizl, Gitl, Aron, and Boris. All of them, the entire family – the parents, the children, who were already adults by then, and the grandchildren – all perished in 1941, except for Buzya and her younger brother Fishl, whose miraculous salvation this testimony describes.

But for now, our story has only reached the end of the 1920s – and the Lord, who in His mercy has hid from us what is revealed to Him, fills this home with peace and joy. Both the grandfather and grandmother were very well aware of Who had preserved and blessed them. They *loved God with all* their *heart and mind*, kept the Jewish traditions, and even under Soviet rule did not conceal their Jewish identity. When praying, the grandfather always donned a *tallit*, or a prayer shawl. In the home, kosher laws were meticulously kept. When a chicken had to be slaughtered, they went to the *shochet*, the ritual slaughterer in Berdichev, over 60 km from Lyubar. "I was proud of my grandfather," remembers Buzya. "He was intelligent, hardworking, and devout. He loved God, and sat reading the Holy Scriptures day and night." In this family, pretty much everyone knew Hebrew, everyone read the Torah, and everyone was awaiting the coming of the Messiah. As the eldest daughter in a big family, Reizl, a white-skinned, blue-eyed beauty (Reizl means sunflower), was taught from childhood to work and help her parents. But even she still studied at a *cheder*, a traditional Jewish elementary school, and knew Hebrew, read the Torah, and later, when Buzya was born, taught her daughter many stories from the Torah. She also told her stories that later, upon becoming a believer, Anna never found in the Torah or Bible, and only later, after coming to Israel, she realized that all these stories were from the oral Torah.

Reizl was not only religious, but she was also a devoted Zionist and was prepared to go to Palestine. Unfortunately, her parents did not support her in this, and the girl decided that she needed to separate from her parents in order to have the chance of going. The issue of marriage arose. Of course, Reizl could only marry another

Jew, and thus it was that Eizik Schmieger, an orphan from Berdichev, appeared in her life. Eizik had no profession, was not particularly religious, and wore a *tallit* only on Pesach. Not being certain whether she was marrying the right man, Reizl went "to inquire" about Eizik from the rabbi in Berdichev, fibbing and saying that they wanted to hire him to work at the shop. The rabbi advised against hiring Eizik as an employee, but then, gazing intently at Reizl, he said out of the blue: "You were really just planning marry him, isn't that so? Well, everything is possible for God. As the Yiddish saying goes, God can make an angel out of a pagan priest." Apparently, somewhere in the heavens where marriages are performed, this marriage was also predetermined. Reizl and Eizik were married.

Anna remembers that though her mama and papa were very, very different, both were full of love for their children. All of Buzya's childhood, up until age 16, was inundated and flooded with this parental warmth and gentleness. She was surrounded by this love until the day when the Germans invaded the city, and death and horror entered the house with them.

Buzya lived in Lyubar until 1933. She went to school there, and finished first grade there. It was, of course, a Jewish school, since there was an excellent Jewish school in pre-war Lyubar. The school's teachers were incredible people, though most of them were die-hard communists, and this is what they taught their pupils. Take Ginda Borisovna Kofman-Dekhtyar, a first grade teacher, for example: It was impossible to find a person in Lyubar who didn't know and love her. Ginda Borisovna always began her first lesson with "The Internationale."[10] First, she read its text in three languages: Ukrainian, Yiddish, and Russian, loudly and distinctly pronouncing the words; then, also in three languages, she would sing "The Internationale" to the first-graders. Then, the children would take hands and raise their voices high – "The Internationale" could not be sung with a lowered head, taught Ginda Borisovna – and they sang together with her. This was how their schooling began, and this is how school began for Buzya, as well.

So it was with this jumble of ideas, from international revolution to faith in the coming of the Messiah, from "The Internationale" to her mama's stories from the Torah, that this girl grew up. When I look back at my own childhood that also took place in Ukraine, many decades after Buzya's, I am well aware that this jumble, this patchwork of ideas around Buzya, was also a blessing. In my lifetime, there was no longer any variety. Decidedly everything around was very firmly cemented into a solid layer of Communist ideology, and I can only be surprised and thank the Lord for His mercy that allowed even me, who grew up among all of this rock-hard, lifeless atheism, to see Him and come to know Him. But in Buzya's lifetime, "The Internationale" somehow thrived alongside the Torah that her mother taught her, and I suppose that no matter how Buzya tried to dissolve into all of this and become the same as everyone, she simply could not. There was still something that distinguished her from the others. There was her mother's faith. The expectation of the Messiah. The Torah. She still knew that there is One to Whom she was indebted for her life. So every morning, upon awakening and arising, she uttered the prayer that later, in Israel, she found in the siddur, *Modeh Ani* - the morning prayer:

מודה אני לפניך מלך חי וקיים

שהחזרת בי נשמתי בהמלה – רבה אמונתך!

I give thanks to You,
living and eternal King,
that you have mercifully returned
my soul within me in compassion.
Great is your faithfulness!

Eizik and Reizl lived in very great poverty. Eizik had to work hard, but his earnings were still not enough, making food scarce, and there was no money for fuel, so in the wintertime, it was so cold in their tiny apartment that the water froze in the tap. In 1927, when Buzya's brother was born – they named him Fishl – Reizl, weakened by the births, could not bear all these trials, and fell ill with heart disease. All the following years are marked in the children's memory by their mother's prayers that the God of Abraham, Isaac, and Jacob would preserve her life and not leave her children orphans.

Life in Lyubar became increasingly difficult. 1933 was a particularly tough year. Some of my readers might yet remember (perhaps from the tales of parents, the way I remember my father's stories) that there was a terrible famine, *Holodomor*, in Ukraine that year. Fishl, who was then 6 years old, still remembers how his feet were swollen from hunger. Then, Eizik, now a salesman, got a job working as the manager of a general store in the village of Velikaya Volitsa. They figured that it would be easier to live (survive!) in that rural community (and we should note that this calculation totally paid off). So, in 1933, the Schmieger family moved from Lyubar to Velikaya Volitsa. A new – and final – chapter in their life had begun.

Velikaya Volitsa was a large, unusually picturesque rural area, with fabulous natural surroundings – but in the entire community, there were only three other Jewish families besides the Schmiegers: the bookkeeper's family, the hairdresser's family, and an elderly retired couple. Lyubar life, where Buzya felt Jewish among a Jewish community, was left behind. Everything had to be restarted from the beginning, and she had to get used to everything new. Of course, there wasn't a Jewish school here, either, and Buzya went to a Ukrainian school. The 8-year-old girl, who by then had already finished first grade in Lyubar, had to go through the first grade again and learn practically everything all over again: She had been studying in a Jewish school and didn't know how to read or write in

Ukrainian. Nonetheless, she surprisingly easily and quickly entered into this new life. She quickly found herself among new friends. Almost immediately, she observed and took note of the girl Nina: careful, neat and tidy, and very beautiful, and notable not only for her outward beauty – blond hair and big hazel eyes – but also for the quiet, inner strength that set her apart from their numerous other peers. Buzya chose this girl for a friend, and this choice ended up being one that lasted many years – a lifetime.

Buzya's parents also really liked Nina, and she soon found herself completely at home in this Jewish household – so much at home that when the matzo had to be baked for Pesach, Reizl invited Nina to help. So much at home that when Buzya's father obtained a winter coat or boots for his growing daughter (many still remember what it meant back then, in our former lives, to acquire a hard-to-come-by winter coat or boots), he also got them for Nina.

These years in Velikaya Volitsa, from 1933 to 1941 – childhood, preadolescence, and the early teen years – were passed specifically with Nina. Nina was the only person with whom Buzya could share her innermost thoughts, the only person who knew everything about her family. She was the only person who knew that the Schmieger's house differed from all the other homes in the village, in that the Word of God, the Torah, was still heard in this home, and that Reizl, who was very knowledgeable of the Torah, frequently told her children stories from the Scriptures. This is how Fishl remembers it: "Mama told us about Abraham, Isaac, and Jacob, about Jacob's 12 sons, about Moses, and King David. I especially loved to hear stories of the Messiah, about how when the Messiah comes, all nations will be subdued by him, peace would come on the earth, and people would cease to wage war. I remember, I once asked mama: So, will only the Jews be saved? Only the Jews will be with God? And then my mama answered me: 'How so? In Motovilovka there are non-Jewish believers who will also be saved.' Who are they, and why? I wondered. 'Because they have no icons, no other images, and they also believe in the only living God. If they live a righteous life, they will also be saved and will be in the Messianic kingdom together with the Jews.'"

Together with Buzya and Fishl, Nina also listened to God's Word – perhaps that was the seed that grew in her heart and thanks to which she didn't abandon Buzya and her family even in the most terrible of times. But before these times and deeds ever came, their friendship was manifested through conversations. I close my eyes and can almost see them before me: two teenage girls, two bright, colorful spots in a verdant meadow. They spoke about everything, and frequently spoke about Buzya's Jewishness, for example. "You know," one of the girls, the one with dark hair and eyes, says thoughtfully to her blond friend, "I'll go to Palestine, and I will send you packages from there." And to this day, as she regularly helps Nina from Jerusalem, Anna remembers these words and is surprised at how God places prophetic words in the mouths of children.

And yet, the most important discussions for them were about the meaning of life, like the one this chapter begins with. Knowing about God and taught to pray to him, Buzya nevertheless longed for God here, on earth. She thirsted for a life here that was already filled with eternity, filled with the infinite preciousness of His presence and distinguished by immortality. "Will we really all die? Then what is all this for? Why did we come into this world? To die?" Buzya thinks about it all the time. She talks with Nina about it. And when she hears from her mother that Enoch was righteous before the Lord, and he didn't diem but was taken alive to God, her heart fills with jubilation. It turns out that everything isn't so hopeless. It turns out that for those who love God, there is a way out: Love God and live a righteous life, and then you won't die – then you'll be with Him in heaven. From that day on, Buzya tried to do only good deeds and help everyone – so as to go to heaven, to God.

And Buzya Schmieger, truly, was just such a girl whom everyone knew by her good deeds. Buzya was a straight-A student, was beloved by her teachers and the pride of the school, and was always ready to help the pupils who needed it. She dreamed about enrolling in an institute and had already begun preparing for it. And how much joy returning to Lyubar for vacation brought her every time, returning to her grandmother and grandfather and the miraculous home on the banks of the Sluch! When the time came, Buzya joined the Komsomol[11] – and it seemed that besides her looks, nothing made her stand out from among the other girls; she was just the same as everyone, differing in no way from the rest. But with heavy soldierly footfalls, a terrible time was already drawing near when she, as well as thousands of others, would be unequivocally made to know that they were "different": *There! A people dwelling alone, not reckoning itself among the nations.*[12]

As before, they lived in abject poverty, but they no longer went hungry. Her father, who worked in procurements, was able to obtain some additional foodstuffs to supplement their meager ration: two pounds of bread and one chicken per week. Her father was also greatly loved by peasants and overseers alike. He could recall virtually the entire village by name, and was equally cordial and honest with everyone. He never wrote anything down ("I never saw him have any sort of notebook, or take any notes"), but he still remembered everything and kept track of it all. Every week, he shipped off two wagons loaded with eggs in cartons – and he was so responsible and careful that in all those years, not a single shipment suffered loss. Soon, her parents were able to buy an *izba,* a peasant's log hut, and Fishl still remembers how mama thanked God for that *izba,* and that no matter how good it was or wasn't, the most important thing was that peace reigned in that home. The family's life passed quietly and happily – loving parents and three children, with Srulik, the youngest, who was born in 1938, the darling of the whole family, of course. The two elder children went to school. When Buzya, upon arriving in Velikaya Volitsa, began attending elementary school, Fishl, who was then six years old, put up a fuss, wanting to be able to study there, too. Reizl went to the director and an agreement was reached so that the next year, Fishl would be accepted early into the first grade. And so it happened that Fishl, though three years younger than his sister, was only one grade behind her. Both were good students: Buzya got straight A's. Fishl's grades, as he himself remembers, were "A's and B's." In 1941, when the war began, Buzya had finished the eighth grade with honors, and Fishl – the seventh.

Fishl remembers those years as the happiest in their family's life. He also remembers the fun winters full of snow and sled-riding, and the marvelous summertime. Every year, with the onset of spring, Fishl went out into the fields where he tilled, plowed, and even planted. He did all this free of charge, because he loved it all so much. Then, with the onset of the summer holidays, he and Buzya would go to Lyubar, to their grandma and grandpa. How they yearned for these trips, which gave them so much joy and happiness! Meeting with grandma and grandpa and chatting with Jewish friends whom they so missed in the village! And then, summer would end – always much faster and sooner than they would have liked – and once again, they returned to Velikaya Volitsa, to their mama and papa, to their younger brother, to school, and to school friends....

There in the village, they remained Jews, but it became increasingly difficult to maintain their Jewish lifestyle. In 1937, Reizl became pregnant with her third child ("perhaps I will give birth to the Messiah," she said), and when the boy Srulik was born in 1938, they had to circumcise him in secret. Besides Nina, no one in the village knew about this secret. Reizl still tried to keep kosher in the home, and still tried to give the chicken to the *shochet* for him to slaughter it according to the rules – but this required mounting efforts and gradually became virtually impossible. Fishl remembers how once, mama gave the chicken to some person to take it to the butcher. The person agreed to do it, took money ostensibly for the butcher, but then butchered the chicken himself and brought it to mama. What do you think Reizl did when she learned about it? She called the person to her, let him keep the money she had given him for the butcher, and gave him the chicken. She was a truly godly person: She was not only firm in strictly observing God's commands, but she also had a soft, gentle, and godly heart.

We will conclude this chapter with one story from pre-war life that Anna-Buzya still remembers with particular emotion. Upon returning home from school once, she caught her mother in the company of two women, one of them from the village, and one from the neighboring village. "I was well aware that mother didn't keep company with gentiles," remembers Buzya. "So it was exceptionally surprising to see her, bright and happy, in conversation with these two women." They came the next day, too, and a day a later. Buzya's mother welcomed them with joy, and her eyes, always beautiful and shining, shined even more strongly with a somehow special inner light. Only years later, when Buzya herself became a believer, did she for the first time realize what had taken place in their home then: These women had shared the gospel with her mother about how Yeshua – Jesus – is the Messiah of Israel, and that faith in Him is faith in the God of Israel. The Holy Spirit touched Reizl very strongly during these meetings, and she accepted Yeshua, believing with all her heart – the way her children later believed – that He was the One for Whom Israel was waiting for so long. But when, a few days later, the nursing mother Reizl contracted mastitis, she said: "I know that I have sinned by recognizing Jesus as Lord and Messiah. Jews should worship only God – and for this, God has punished me with mastitis." With that, the story seemed to end – but nothing is ever an accident with God. He never forgets anything, and what was sown then brought forth fruit in the heart of Buzya and her brother Fishl: *For as the rain comes down, and the snow from heaven, and do not return there, but water the earth, and make it bring forth and bud, that it may give seed to the sower and bread to the eater, so shall My word be that goes forth from My mouth; it shall not return to Me void, but it shall accomplish what I please, and it shall prosper in the thing for which I sent it.*[13] The Word of God completed its work in the heart and life of Buzya and Fishl – but the road there lay through ascending Mount Moriah, through such suffering, such sorrow and pain that, as in the story of Isaac, the angels in the heavens wept and mourned together with those heading to the slaughter....

Chapter 2

THE RAISED KNIFE

Let the groaning of the prisoner come before You;
According to the greatness of Your power
Preserve those who are appointed to die.
(Psalm 79:11)

"I was 16 years old when the horror began." This
is how Anna's written recollections shift to the
events about which she is unable to speak to this
day. "It was as if the sun had turned back and
gone the other direction, and everything grew
dark." The Germans advanced rapidly; already
within a few days after the beginning of World
War II, a few of the neighboring villages were
being bombed, and the Germans entered their
village just a few weeks after the war began. Some
people managed to evacuate during those weeks.
Buzya's family stayed because of her: Buzya, the
Komsomolka, had been taken away along with
her teachers and fellow pupils to dig trenches,
and her parents could not bring themselves to
leave without their daughter. Besides that, the
ones who left were the more well-to-do families
who were able to instantly pay for transportation.
Eizik and Reizl, who could barely make ends
meet, did not have that sort of money and were
unable to leave, at least so quickly. By the time

Buzya returned, the village was occupied by the Germans, and evacuation was no longer possible.

As I read back through Anna's writings, I realize that the distress and shock of these first days and weeks of war weren't caused merely by the physical fear and suffering, but also, to an enormous extent, by the sudden and rapid change in – betrayal by! – those who until recently had seemed to be close, loving friends. *For it is not an enemy who reproaches me; then I could bear it. Nor is it one who hates me who has exalted himself against me; then I could hide from him. But it was you, a man my equal, my companion and my acquaintance.*[14] In the very first days following the German invasion, many of their fellow villagers changed unrecognizably. When all the Jews living in the village were ordered not to appear outside their homes without the six-pointed star, to their colossal amazement, so many Ukrainians sincerely rejoiced over this. For example, Buzya's first teacher, whom she had loved since her very first day at the Velikaya Volitsa school and whom she had admired all these years, almost immediately became a prefect. Going out to the central square, she delivered a speech to the people: "Brothers and sisters! How happy we are, how many years we have awaited this moment!" One can only attempt to imagine what must have transpired in the heart of a 16-year-old girl – who loved the world and people and sincerely believed that she was also beloved of those near her – upon suddenly finding herself betrayed by all those whom she had trusted. In those first weeks of the occupation, when they still remained in the village, Buzya was horrified and astonished to make increasingly new "discoveries." There was, for example, Zhenya Shultz – her first childhood heartthrob, who not so long ago had fawned over her during recess and accompanied her home every day from school. He suddenly became a *polizei* who began zealously – and most frighteningly of all, completely voluntarily! – fulfilling his frightening duties. Or take Petro Rybak, another fellow pupil, who also went to serve – also voluntarily! – in the *Ukrainische Hilfspolizei*, as the police in Nazi-occupied Ukraine were called. This was the most astonishing thing of all: No one had coerced them. They themselves joined the *polizei* of their own volition. And when the *polizei* arrived a couple months later to collect the Jews of Velikaya Volitsa and take them to Lyubar, it was those same former friends – Petro Rybak and Zhenya Shultz – who came with the wagons that were taking them to certain death.

During those first couple months, though they were grueling and joyless, some spark of hope remained that they could survive and get through this terrible time. Eizik and Buzya went to work every day – they were driven into forced labor, and they themselves did all they could to try to earn something to live on. But already, rumors began circulating about the shootings of Jews in Lyubar. About how the youngest, educated, and intelligent had been loaded onto carts and driven 5 kilometers outside Lyubar, into the Peschanoye district, where they had all been shot. Two weeks later, this firing squad was repeated – and after that, virtually no Jews were left in Lyubar. Unable and unwilling to believe these rumors, Buzya's mother sent her to Lyubar, disguised as a peasant, to find out about her grandfather, grandmother, and the rest of the family. Upon her return, Buzya reported that grandfather's house was empty, that all the Jewish homes were empty, and that the Jews were not being sent to Palestine, as the rumors had been at first, but were being shot.

In August, after all of Lyubar's Jews had been shot, they began to haul in all the Jews from the surrounding region and villages, seeking out everyone who remained there or was perhaps in hiding. It was announced that if anyone hid Jews, their whole family would be shot, whereas if someone turned a Jew in, he would be rewarded with 500 Reichsmarks. The dreaded day came that they had anticipated all these weeks: One morning, a policeman came to them and said: Don't take a single step outside your house; today you will be sent to Lyubar. And then came the wagon on which those former fellow pupils – Petro Rybak and Zhenya Shultz – took them to their death. Are there words to describe the horror of when those you considered friends come not only to take away your life, but the lives of the people dearest to you?

Recalling that terrifying day when her family's life finally screeched to a halt, when the cart with the *polizei* came to take them to Lyubar, Anna also remembers how she, taught from childhood to pray and seek God, turned in the direction of

Jerusalem and, through tears, began to pray and weep. Strangely enough, though she prayed for a long time, no one stopped her. No one shouted or beat or hurried her. And then, while sitting in the cart, scarf thrown over her head, she unmistakably seemed to hear His voice: "Take your ribbons and scarves. You will live, you will grow out your hair, and everything you planned to do before the war, you will do." It was as if a stony weight had lifted off her heart. Now, despite all the gloom and fear all around, she had heard His voice, and she had His promise to cling to. All the way to Lyubar, the entire 16-kilometer journey, she conversed with God....

The Lord is my shepherd; I shall not want. **He** *makes me to lie down in green pastures; He leads me beside the still waters.... Yea, though I walk through the valley of the shadow of death, I will fear no evil; for* **You** *are with me;* **Your** *rod and* **Your** *staff, they comfort me.*[15]

Have you ever paid attention to the breathtaking peculiarity of this psalm – perhaps one of the most famous and well-known of all 150 psalms? Have you ever noticed that while He tends us *in green pastures* and *beside still waters,* the Lord is **He** for us. But when one enters *the valley of the shadow of death,* the Lord becomes **You.** There, in this *shadow of death,* a person comes to know the Lord face to face. And for Buzya, who entered this *shadow of death,* the Lord truly became **You** for her from that moment on. Ever after, she unceasingly sought Him in her heart, and in her heart, she heard His voice.

Did I really hear it? She often doubted it, since after all, it was His quiet voice speaking within her, and it was very difficult to trust Him, to see with the heart and not the eyes, to believe in God's promises despite everything that was happening around her. It was difficult to believe, difficult to live by *the evidence of things not seen,* when what you are seeing is so terrifying…. They were brought to the regional police station, but already the next morning, they were taken from there to the Jewish school – to that same school Buzya had attended in first grade. By the time the Schmieger family was brought there, several hundred people were already there. Everyone who had survived in Lyubar after the mass shootings, or who hadn't been in their homes, but had hidden somewhere and had now been found, or who had been living in villages like the Schmiegers was being brought there. Even before arriving at the school, they could sense the stifled air. The building was crammed full. People were standing or, at best, sitting on the floor; there was nowhere to lie down. To their horror, they now received the final confirmation of what they had previously guessed: They learned that none of the Chaim Rabinovich family – their family – had survived, that no one was left alive from that whole large family. Everything that was happening seemed like an endless nightmare where you try with all your might to wake up, but instead find yourself in an even more dreadful place. In real life, it would seem, so many terrifying events just could not be happening all at once. The news of the death of all

– all! – of their relatives was mixed with the awfulness and stench of that overstuffed, once-beloved building; with the smell of bodies, tears, and dirt; with the terrible torment of one's own powerlessness to help those you love, who are suffering right next to you....

And still they continued to bring people in. When the school was already absolutely overflowing – so that it was impossible to pack anyone else in there, let alone for people to sit or stand – they were taken to another, larger building on the outskirts of Lyubar: an orphanage. Prior to the Bolshevik Revolution, there had been a large monastery there. Afterward, the monastery had been dismantled and its buildings refitted as an orphanage. And now, in this monastery with its long and longer halls and sundry rooms and cells, situated on two stories, a ghetto was set up for the Jews.

The entire Schmieger family – the parents, Buzya, and her two brothers, 13-year-old Fishl and 4-year-old Srulik – were stuffed into one of the rooms of this orphanage. Some 50 people were stuffed into every room, which had originally been monastic cells, essentially, where one or maximum two monks had resided. It was impossible to sit down, so they even slept standing up. There was nothing to eat; there was no food whatsoever in the ghetto. Sometimes, tender-hearted peasants came, risking their lives, and brought boiled potatoes to the ghetto. But it was impossible to feed hundreds of prisoners with a few pails of potatoes, and people died daily: from hunger, despair, beatings, and from the inhumane conditions in which they were kept. Nursling infants died, unnourished by their mothers' empty breasts. The elderly died, unable to withstand the conditions in which they found themselves. For the rest of her life, Anna has suffered nighttime flashbacks, hearing the cries of an elderly man on whom heartless beasts tested the measure of human endurance. Every day, they would beat him mercilessly, then shut him up in a cupboard. The next day, this cruel procedure would be repeated, until death liberated the unfortunate man from his torment. And then – a new victim; again – the beatings, the wails, and moans…. This was all done very systematically; they were learning brutality in step with a methodical plan. To this day, these cries and moans haunt Anna's nights.

Those who were stronger, younger, and could withstand more were herded out in the mornings to work under a guard, barely alive after enduring yet another nightmare of a night. And though people had no strength left to work, still, many envied them: This at least gave them the opportunity to leave the ghetto. Inside, the ghetto was completely unbearable: the stench, the crowding, the groans, and the cries – especially the cries of the children. In these terrible conditions, each day seemed to stretch into an eternity in hell.

"It is impossible to write about it, impossible even to think about it, and yet it is necessary! It must be remembered; it must not be forgotten!" Anna writes in her recollections. "Every day lasted a year. Any minute, we expected to be herded to the firing line. People would fall on each other's necks, saying their goodbyes, kissing, and weeping out loud – we were waiting for the end." From time to time, Ukrainian men came to the ghetto, bringing their Jewish wives and children and handing them over. Anyone who had Jewish blood to the fourth generation was considered a Jew. Sometimes perfectly indigenous-looking children were brought in – towheaded and pug-nosed – but there had been a Jewish grandmother or grandfather somewhere back in their family tree. The 500 Reichsmarks, promised as a reward to whomever gave up a Jew, was a temptation for them, and an active hunt went on throughout the rural areas, seeking out anyone a reward could be obtained for.

Seeing these people who were prepared to betray even their own families for 500 Reichsmarks, Buzya thanked God again and again for her schoolmate Nina Koval. Every week, she came to the ghetto from afar, from Velikaya Volitsa, to sustain them. Buzya will never forget this help and support. Nina was the only joy for the Schmieger family during those months. That love, care, and even just food that they had until very recently so generously shared with Nina – all of it returned to them when they needed it the most. Did Reizl, strengthening her gaunt children with the home-baked bread that Nina brought every week – did she remember the words of Ecclesiastes? *Cast your bread upon the waters, for you will find it after many days.*[16] Today it is clear to me, just how it was evidently also clear to Reizl there, in the ghetto, that the Word of the living God that Nina had heard in their home did not return void; it fell *on good ground and yielded a crop.*[17]

But even with this blessed assistance and sustenance, their strength was waning. They realized that the end was near and prepared themselves for it as best they could. Anna remembers how in the atrocious, completely anti-sanitary conditions of the ghetto, where there was nothing to drink, no drinking water, let alone anything to wash with, she knew that when the end came and she saw the Lord, she must stand before him clean and fresh. So in the mornings, she would gather the condensation from the sweaty window to wash her face. "All of those terrible days, I cried out to God," recalls Anna. "It's tradition to seek God with washed face and hands, but there wasn't even any water to drink there, let alone to wash one's hands or face. What could be done? There were over 100 people in our room, in such cramped quarters and stuffiness that the window would get very fogged up, and in the mornings, I would gather this precious moisture from the window to wash my face before prayer. I feared God and awaited help from Him alone." At the ghetto, people did not scorn various methods of survival: For example, the *polizei* agreed to let the children out, who would go into the villages, begging or simply stealing, and returning to their parents in the ghetto, bringing them gold and rings. This was all done in order to take these trophies to pay the fortune teller who appeared not far off, in hope of hearing words of comfort and false promises from her. "I did not expect help except from the Almighty, and there is not enough paper to describe all the miracles and signs He revealed to me in His mercy. Here are just a few examples.

"Rumors circulated that those families whom peasants would assume responsibility for would be released into their custody and let live. With the permission of the guards and *polizei*, I also went to the village to make such an appeal. It so happened that at this very same time, a high-ranking policeman came in. He obviously fancied the 16-year-old Jewish girl and, upon leaving, he told me: 'Tonight you'll come out to me.' 'No,' I said. 'In that case, I'll bring you out by force,' he said. 'Then by force it will be,' I said. We parted – but with what a heavy heart I returned 'home' to mama. I don't remember how I got there; I came and told all to mama, and then ran to the window. There was a big window in the corridor, and I raised my eyes to the One from Whom my help comes – to my God. My prayer was strong, tearful, so sincere, and so passionate – and the Lord showed me a miracle in response to it: I watched as one after another, right next to each other, two meteors rose in the sky. Before that, I had often seen falling stars, but I had never seen one travel upward, especially two at once. Then I understood that it was a sign – an answer to my prayer, that He would preserve me; but only later, looking back, did I understand that God had shown me in this miraculous, supernatural way that He would save not only me, but also my brother.

"That night, the *polizei* came to look for me with a lantern. I was sleeping on my knees next to mama, covered with her scarf – and covered by God's hand! Nothing happened; not only did they not find me, but I didn't even hear any of it. How I thanked God for His mercy!

"Almost every day, one *polizei* would come in to me, giving me a loaf of bread and a piece of *salo*, the traditional Ukrainian food that is cured pork fat. I don't know who it was; I never knew him before, nor after. Our family would eat the bread, and I would throw the salo in the river when we were brought out, fearful of sinning. After the war, when I returned to Lyubar, I tried to look for him to thank him for his kindness, but was never able to find him. People said that he had been sent away, that he had been sentenced to 10 years in prison. I think he was from a family of believers, which is why he had helped me.

"The *polizei* – we saw no one except for them, it was only the *polizei* who dealt with the Jews – cared for nothing except their own pleasure and profiteering. They took anything of some valuable or simply good quality away from the prisoners and entertained themselves with torture and torment. The rooms were connected via long hallways. Along these hallways, the people were driven – sometimes completely naked – from room to room, while the *polizei* roughly and vulgarly searched them in hopes of discovering something of value: gold, silver, or valuables. By night, the drunken *polizei* would bring girls out into a long corridor, raping and ridiculing them. But even in this, the hand of the Lord was with me: Miraculously, He preserved me and allowed no one to defile me."

Fishl, Buzya's brother, recalls: "I remember that a few days before the end, mama woke up in the morning and wept very bitterly. I also began to cry and said to her: Mama, why are you crying? She told me that she had seen grandfather in a dream, lying dead, with a radiance over him – the hallowed Kingdom of Heaven – while the *polizei* beat me and Buzya. They beat us and beat us, but we were still alive. And then mama said: 'If there is a God in heaven, you and Buzya will remain alive – only you two will survive!' And then she added: 'Children, when the two of you are left alone, go to Jerusalem.'" Today, over 60 years after that night, with Buzya and Fishl the only survivors from among all of the 500 Jews who were kept in the ghetto, and with both living in Israel, can there be any doubt that there is a God in heaven?

The cries, the moans, the weeping – the nightmare of the Lyubar ghetto went on for nearly three months. It seemed like it would never end, and death felt like a more welcome escape and salvation. The suffering and torment the prisoners were subjected to were such than many began to view death as deliverance. Then again, no one offered them any other way out. On 30 October

1941, after over two months of torture and abuse, *polizei* arrived at the ghetto from the neighboring Chudnov Region. They came to conduct a "campaign": the total extermination of all the prisoners in the Lyubar ghetto. On the evening of 30 October, all of them – both the Lyubar and the Chudnov *polizei* – "celebrated" the upcoming event with a monstrous drunken brawl, drowning with vodka the remnants of human feelings which, most likely, kept some of them awake at night. The next day, on 31 October, before dawn early in the morning, all the men were sent out under guard to dig pits. At nine in the morning, all the rest of the people were brought out and lined up in the long corridor, then led out. A *polizei* was stationed after every fifth person. All of Buzya's family stood in line, as well – her parents, Buzya herself, and her two younger brothers. No one had any doubts about where they were being led. Everyone knew that this was their final journey. It seemed like it was all over; from where could salvation come? And could it even come?

And Abraham stretched out his hand and took the knife to slay his son....[18]

This example might not seem very appropriate; perhaps this biblical parallel is causing you some indignation. In the one case, Abraham, a righteous man beloved of God, is willing to sacrifice his own son out of obedience and loyalty to God. In our story, a pack of lost, ungodly humans in the guise of policemen are leading perfectly innocent people to the slaughter. But it's very important to understand that I'm not comparing Abraham and the *polizei*, but **those being slain**. Similar to how Isaac was led to the altar solely because he was the beloved son, because he was infinitely precious to his father – in exactly the same way, the prisoners of the Lyubar ghetto, just like the millions of other prisoners in other ghettos and concentration camps during those terrible years, were led out to be killed solely because they were Jews, because they were Israel, a people whom God has called His son and firstborn, and who are infinitely dear to their Father. In Genesis 22, in describing the sacrifice of Isaac, the Scriptures do not make us privy to either Abraham's emotions, nor the feelings of Isaac; nevertheless, since the Bible says that this test, this *temptation,* was first and foremost aimed at Abraham, it is specifically the goings-on in the spirit of the father that usually interest those reading and studying this story. But have you ever considered what the son, led to be slain, must have felt in those minutes? At which point on this path did Isaac realize that he was going to his death, to be slain? What did he think, what did he feel on this journey – a journey whose every step irrevocably brought him closer to the altar? Did he realize that he was being led to be slain **only because** he was beloved of his father and infinitely precious to him? And if he did understand this, did he regret that his father loved him **in such a way**? Did he desire at that moment for the father's love for him to be not so vast, for his father to love him less? And can we even try to imagine what Isaac felt at that moment, when the hand extending a knife over him was stopped at the very last moment?

The two stars that Buzya saw during her prayer had long had their path prepared for them by the Lord. Here are some lines from her remembrances: "On 31 October, at six in the morning, they took all the men, including my father, to dig a pit in Peschanoye. At nine in the morning, they lined us all up. My mama stood in front with my five-year-old little brother, and I and my brother Fishl, who was three years younger than me, were behind them. Along the entire hallway, the monks' cells were all tightly closed. Then suddenly, I saw something: The door to one of them was ajar. In that instant, it was clear to me that this door had been opened by Him for us, and that our path lay there. I took my brother by the hand, and it seemed as if it were not me, but the hand of the Heavenly Father directing us from on high. And though deadly danger was all around, I knew that we were in His hand – and therefore in safety. As if in a dream, I pushed on the door, and we found ourselves in a cell. All of this took mere seconds, but glancing back, turning it over and over in my mind as if in slow motion, once again seeing all of it play out before me, and reliving all of it innumerable times, I cannot fathom how they didn't see us, and how we managed to do it. There is only one explanation: The Lord shut the eyes of everyone who was nearby, for with His hand, He was leading us and preparing us both for salvation.

"We found ourselves in a cell with a small window. My brother – he was 13 years old – easily climbed out through the window, whereas for me, a fully-formed 16-year-old girl, this seemed nigh impossible. How could I fit through that tiny window? And then, the second miracle happened that day – the day of salvation – the second miracle within those few minutes. I'm not sure how, but the window seemed to give way, widen, and let me through." In the blink of an eye, they found themselves on the other side of the fence, among the gardens on the banks of the Sluch. Somewhere there, on the opposite side, the innocent victims were being led out to be slain – their loved ones were being taken to be shot – while the brother and sister, trembling from shock and fear, saved and led by God's hand, stood beneath the ghetto windows. The knife raised over them had been stopped at the very last moment – and just like in the story of Isaac, it was stopped by His hand. And though at first Buzya, sobbing, cried out to her brother: "No, I don't want to live, let's go back and die with them all, why should we live, if they won't be with us," the Lord had His plan for their lives, and so He placed His answer in the mouth of the 13-year-old boy: "Do you really think," said Fishl, crying and embracing her, "that it will be easier for our mama if all three of her children are shot? Let's go, Buzya; we'll trust God. If this is His will, we'll end up with good people and will live – and if not, we will end up with bad ones, and die." And so they left.

Thus, the mother's dream began to come true; God's promises were fulfilled; Buzya's prayers were answered; two stars didn't fall, but ascended to heaven. Where would their journey lead them now?

***

At this point, I should probably pause for a moment. This story was conceived as a testimony, a story of salvation and coming to faith, and in approaching Anna's recollections, I very clearly imagined to myself that fine line, that indubitable watershed moment in this story at which believers in Jesus (Yeshua) meet Yeshua Himself. In my years as a believer, I have heard numerous testimonies, and in each of them, just as in my own story, there is always this unmistakable, compelling boundary that lies between life without God and life with God. This line is simply impossible to miss – just as, for example, when standing on the seashore, it is impossible to be mistaken about where the shore ends and the water begins. In my life, just as in the lives of many other believers, this boundary between "before" and "after" is just as distinct and indubitable as the line between the land and the water. However, the more I read through Anna's remembrances – in which she writes that even before she met up with believers and came to faith in Yeshua, she "feared God and awaited help from Him alone" – the more amazed I became upon realizing that Buzya, having not yet met Yeshua, having not yet accepted Him as Lord and Messiah, nonetheless constantly sought God.

Moreover, her relationship with Him was so deep and firm that even in the midst of this whole nightmare, horror, and suffering, God remained alive and real to her, in some sense much more real than everything that was happening around her. So, completely unexpectedly, I suddenly realized that this was virtually the most important thing that the Lord was showing me in this story: this very smooth, almost imperceptible transition from Buzya's prayers and appeals to God in the ghetto, when she did not yet know Yeshua and yet where God was completely alive and real to her, to the acceptance of Yeshua as the Messiah whom her family had waited for and Who did not cancel or change, but only strengthened her faith in the God of Israel. Apparently, in some sense, it's specifically for this reason that this book is being written: The Lord wants to show us all that behind the visible façade of the story of the "conversion" of two Jewish children to Christianity, as must evidently be behind many other similar stories that occurred during the Holocaust, a great mystery is concealed. The mystery of the breaking of the seals of a Book. The mystery of a Messiah Who is appearing – Who is revealing Himself!

In the age of digital cameras, clearly few of us remember how ordinary, non-digital photographs were developed in the (not so distant) past: The film was placed in a special solution, and sometime later, at first the contours would appear, and then the finer details of the latent image. I myself have never done this, so the entire process has always seemed like some sort of incredibly mysterious, almost mystical undertaking to me. It seems completely incredible that, on the one hand, the image is already there; it already exists in its entirety, perfectly imprinted on the film. The complex chemical process changes nothing about this image and adds nothing to it; it only develops, reveals, and puts on display what was already there. On the other hand, though only this one step separates us from seeing completely what is imprinted on the photograph, without doing this step, without developing the film, we will never discover what is pictured.

The mystery of a sealed – and unsealed – book about which I am now going to write is in some sense very similar to the process of developing photographs. There is a surprising passage of Scripture that has troubled my heart for many years:

The whole vision has become to you like the words of a book that is sealed, which men deliver to one who is literate, saying, "Read this, please." And he says, "I cannot, for it is sealed." Then the book is delivered to one who is illiterate, saying, "Read this, please." And he says, "I am not literate."[19]

What is this book the prophet is speaking about? Let's start with the beginning of the verse – *the whole vision*. We aren't dealing with some specific prophecy, but with a global picture, a vision and understanding of everything that God has done and is doing in the history of mankind, about God's universal plan of salvation – about what begins in Genesis 3, after the fall, and concludes in the book of Revelation. So I believe that we are reading about that very same sealed Book that we see in Chapter 5 of Revelation: the book of God's plan for all of mankind.

And I saw in the right hand of Him who sat on the throne a scroll written inside and on the back, sealed with seven seals. Then I saw a strong angel proclaiming with a loud voice, "Who is worthy to open the scroll and to loose its seals?" And no one in heaven or on the earth or under the earth was able to open the scroll, or to look at it. So I wept much, because no one was found worthy to open and read[a] the scroll, or to look at it.[20]

Some might say that this parallel is very, very forced, that these are two completely different books and there is no connection between them. But do you know that, surprising as it may be, in all the Scriptures, there are only three sealed books? Besides the verses from Isaiah and Revelation quoted above, the prophet Daniel speaks of another book, about which the prophet is given a very unequivocal command: *"But you, Daniel, shut up the words, and **seal the book** until the time of the end; many shall run to and fro, and knowledge shall increase."*[21] There is no doubt whatsoever that the sealing of Daniel's book, like the sealing of the book in Revelation, comes in a completely prophetic context; dare we say that Isaiah's sealed book is in no way linked to these two prophetic books? I am profoundly convinced that all three books are not only linked, but that they are one and the same book – the book of

God's plans for mankind, revealed in a vision to Daniel as sealed by God and shown in a vision to John as unsealed by Yeshua.

So, we see this shut book, this sealed scroll of God's plan, and it is delivered to *one who is literate, saying, "Read this, please." And he says, "I cannot, for it is sealed."* I have meditated on the significance of this strange picture: Who is it that knows how to read, but for some reason receives this book sealed? And only very recently, the Lord revealed it to me – and as it always happens when He Himself grants a revelation, the truth He shows instantly becomes so obvious that you simply wonder how you never saw it before. But anyway, the Lord showed me that the *literate* one is Israel: Our people are not only literate concerning the *Tanakh* – the Hebrew Scriptures, God's Word – but are also able to read God's handwriting in history. We are taught to recognize God, His signature, and His plan in events around us. And it would seem, who else should read this book, but the one who is literate? But that's just the issue: Specifically for the literate, the book is sealed. As we read in the prophet Daniel, it is sealed by God Himself or, at least, by His direct command, and as we read in John's writings, it can be unsealed only by God Himself. In Revelation, we are told with perfect clarity Who is the One that can remove this seal, the One Who has the ability to unseal this Book: *But one of the elders said to me, "Do not weep. Behold, the Lion of the tribe of Judah, the Root of David, has prevailed to open the scroll and to loose its seven* seals."[22] The Greek text here is clear that the Lion of the tribe of Judah has not simply prevailed generally and can now unseal this Book in addition to His other victories. It doesn't read: *"has prevailed and can also open."* Don't you see? His very victory consists of the fact that the Book can now be opened, and the seals removed: *has prevailed to open the scroll.* And as soon as Yeshua removes the seals and opens this Book, the *literate* are now able to read it. Nothing new is added to this Book, but similar to how a photographic film is developed, everything that latently existed before is now revealed for the first time, becoming visible and apparent.

As we will soon see, this is the story of our two heroes, Buzya and Fishl. Then again, is it their story alone? The same thing also occurred with the Apostle Paul – Rabbi Shaul – who, as we know, studied the Torah and Scriptures his whole life and who, unquestionably, was *literate* even before his meeting with Yeshua – but until Yeshua Himself removed the seals for him, Shaul could not read this scroll. At that moment when Yeshua appeared and revealed Himself to him, when the seals were removed from this Book, then was the Book read. I suppose that for most of my readers, it is perfectly obvious just how ludicrous of an anachronism is the traditional view of Paul's conversion from Judaism to Christianity: Once upon a time, there was a good, but deluded Jew who zealously read and tried to fulfill the Torah, but meanwhile had no relationship whatsoever with the living God –

then suddenly, upon meeting Jesus on the road to Damascus, he understood everything, made a decisive break from Israel and the Torah, changed his spots, and became a normal person and an excellent Christian (Orthodox, Catholic, Pentecostal – depending on what denomination is laying forth these views). Naturally, this beloved image does not stand up to either biblical, nor historical criticism: Shaul could not become a Christian in the sense that we understand it today, if for no other reason than at the moment he met Yeshua, such a word didn't even exist (the first time this term appears is in Acts 11:26). And nonetheless, it's indubitable that after his meeting with Yeshua, a change occurred not only in his heart, but also in the head of this *literate* scribe and Pharisee. Have you ever considered what went on with Shaul during those three days that he spent, shocked and blinded, in fasting and prayer in Damascus, on **Straight** Street, before Ananias was sent to him? What did he think about during his imposed standstill, while rethinking – straightening out – his life and his convictions, without the ability to physically read, and therefore mentally paging through the Scriptures on which he was nurtured? They had always been his life, the meaning and the foundation for his existence, but now, to his incredible bewilderment, the One Who three days ago he had been perfectly confident was not there, simply could not be there, was appearing on these pages, revealed before his inner gaze. With incredible insight and credibility, Shaul should have realized that somewhere, he had got it wrong. That the selfsame Yeshua Whom he had considered a deceiver and seducer, Who, in his opinion, the entire *Tanakh* bore witness against, was in fact the Son of God and true Messiah. That not only did His teachings not contradict the Torah, but on the contrary, they revealed its true meaning. Let's meditate together on this situation: No new texts or documents fell to Shaul from heaven; it was the same Scripture, the same text of the *Tanakh* that he had read his entire life, but simply now seen, understood, and read in a completely new light. This is the unsealing of the Book, the revealing of what previously existed, but until now had simply been invisible. This is the removal of those seven seals we read about in Revelation: At the moment when His sovereign hand removes the seals, the *literate* simply cannot help but read this Book.

The story that we are following – the story of Buzya and Fishl – is about this same sealed Book and a Messiah Who **reveals** Himself, Who changes everything about their lives, yet does not change any part of the text of this Book itself.

Chapter 3

A LAMB, AS THOUGH IT HAD BEEN SLAIN...

So I pastured the flock
doomed to slaughter.
(Zachariah 11:7) NASB

The brother and sister found themselves in the monastery gardens on the banks of the Sluch. There was no time to stop and think, and first, they ran over the bridge across the Sluch, and then along its banks, sprinting from vegetable patch to vegetable patch and trying, while on the run, to guess where to go, which house to turn to. Where would they be received, and not given up? Buzya mentally calculated that they needed to look for a poor, wretched hut, thinking that the impoverished would be more merciful, and that in just such a place, they might be able to count on compassion. This was her human reasoning, but *as the heavens are higher than the earth, so are My ways higher than your ways, and My thoughts than your thoughts,*[23] says the Lord. Not by their reasoning, but by His plan, He led them in His ways, and led them by His own hand to the house where salvation had been prepared for them....

There is a remarkable passage of Scripture that I recall every time the topic of believers during the Holocaust comes up – those who saved Jews or those who didn't. *Thus says the Lord my God, "Pasture the flock doomed to slaughter. Those who buy them slay them and go unpunished, and each of those who sell them says, 'Blessed be the Lord, for I have become rich!'"*[24] On that October day long ago, the brother and sister were well aware that they were *doomed to slaughter;* they could be slain by people who would go *unpunished;* they could be sold and make people *rich.* But they didn't know whether they had hope of finding anyone who would be willing to *pasture the flock doomed to slaughter,* and not kill or sell them. The only One they could trust and whose help they could count on was the Lord Himself. With all their heart, they believed that He would not leave them, and they were proven right.

Time after time in the New Testament, Yeshua Himself testifies that He can do only what the Father does: *Most assuredly, I say to you, the Son can do nothing of Himself, but what He sees the Father do; for whatever He does, the Son also does in like manner.*[25] If even He, God's Son, to Whom *all authority... in heaven and on earth*[26] has been given, *can do nothing of Himself, but what He sees the Father do,* then what does that say about us ordinary believers? The Father expects us to do the same works that He Himself does – and therefore, in my opinion, He would not have commanded us to *pasture the flock doomed to slaughter* if He Himself didn't also promise in His Word: *And I will feed the flock of slaughter.*[27] The brother and sister who thought that they were left utterly alone in the world were in His hands, and **He Himself pastured them.** He Himself guided them to a place with people who loved Him and who kept His commands. Had they entered any other house that day, their lives could have been instantly cut off – had they ended up in the hands of those who *slay... and go unpunished,* or would be happy to grow rich from selling them. But led and directed by Him, they came to the only place, to the only people in that city who, like the Father, were willing to *pasture* and save *the flock doomed to slaughter*. In this sense, in Buzya and Fishl's story, we see only one more of the countless testaments to His faithfulness. When we are absolutely helpless and truly willing to place ourselves in His hands (sometimes, sadly enough, only because there is nothing else we can do) – that is when His *strength is made perfect* in our weakness,[28] and He Himself enters our hopeless circumstances. It's then that the seemingly totally impassable *mountains* of obstacles *melt like wax at the presence of the Lord.*[29] It's then that we experience what Buzya and Fishl experienced that day: *He sent from above, He took me; He drew me out of many waters. He delivered me from my strong enemy, from those who hated me, for they were too strong for me. They confronted me in the day of my calamity, but the Lord was my support.*[30]

For approximately 2 kilometers, they walked along the Sluch, at last finding themselves next to the large courtyard of an apparently affluent family, with a solid new house faced in brick. "We didn't plan to go in there; we wanted to continue on." But at that moment, a young, light-haired woman – the mistress of the house – came out of her home, saw the children, and walked toward them.

The brother and sister saw the Ukrainian woman approaching them. All of their insides froze, and they themselves froze in their tracks. Can you imagine this instant? A person is approaching you, and you know that your life or death depends on his or her decision. You have probably faced situations in your life when some extremely important answer depended on the decision of one person – about an apartment, a school, or a trip. In human terms, it's a very strange – and not at all comfortable – feeling, when you know that something highly momentous to your fate depends on some stranger. But in this case, their very lives depended on this unfamiliar woman's decision. Who was she? Why exactly was she heading toward them?

This is how one of Anna Sanevich's daughters remembers this day, based on what her mother told her, naturally: "Mama went out of the house and saw that a friend and her son were coming into our courtyard. Mama was very happy and went out to meet her. But when she got a little closer, she suddenly saw that it wasn't her friend at all, but two Jewish children, a 16-year-old girl and a boy of 12 or 13 with her." Can you imagine? Among the piles of various documents and recollections, I ran across the page with this story almost by accident – and stopped short from delight and thankfulness to God. I truly love to hear testimonies of an event from an outside perspective, especially when they reveal what was occuring that went unseen by the situation's beneficiaries. As believers, we are called to go through this life on *the evidence of things not seen,*[31] and much of the time we live without seeing or knowing what is going on "behind the scenes," or through what or whom the Lord has changed our circumstances. But then again, what a blessing it is to have the opportunity to suddenly, unexpectedly take a peek into these *things not seen,* to find out exactly how a divine intervention occurred in the visible circumstances, to observe how the Lord moved certain people to do something that becomes a complete miracle for someone else. Take the story about Phillip and the eunuch from the Book of Acts, for example. *Now an angel of the Lord spoke to Philip, saying, "Arise and go toward the south along the road which goes down from Jerusalem to Gaza." This is desert. So he arose and went.*[32] There is no doubt that when Phillip found himself next to the eunuch returning in his chariot from Jerusalem, where he was able to interpret the verses from Isaiah to him and share the gospel about Yeshua with him, this was undoubtedly all a miracle for the eunuch, who knew nothing about what God had told Philip – *Arise and go... along the road which goes down from Jerusalem to Gaza* – and a totally unexpected one, at that. However, the Lord, Whose *eyes are open to all the ways of the sons of men,*[33] is very well aware of who and when to send on these paths:

completely deliberately, with the image of her friend coming toward her, He had prompted Anna Sanevich to hurry to meet the two Jewish children.

And now we return to our protagonists, to once again "peek" at this story from their eyes. "Our appearance was such that there could be no doubt where we had come from," recalls Buzya. "By our clothing, our faces, and especially our eyes, it was perfectly clear that we were Jews who had escaped from the ghetto. We were expecting just about any reaction: for her to start calling for the *polizei*, to hand us over to death; or that she would demand that we immediately leave her yard, so as there not to be any unpleasantness; or, at best, that she would allow us to continue onward, pretending not to have seen us; or perhaps even – in our boldest imagination – would hint at which house it would be best to turn to. The only thing we didn't anticipate was to hear her tell us herself, in Ukrainian: "Children, come into the house."

What did it mean for this woman to accept Jews into her house? She had four children of her own, three girls and a boy, and all of them were sitting at the table when Buzya and Fishl entered. If Jews were discovered in their home, the entire family would be shot. Anna and Ivan Sanevich, the owners of the house, were well aware of this; they understood that from this very moment, by saving these Jewish children, they were risking the lives of their own children – but they were believers who knew God's Word. They knew that only the one who *loses his life for My sake will save it,*[34] and that *a grain of wheat* must fall *into the ground and die.*[35] They knew that without the crucifixion, there would never have been the resurrection, and they knew that the Savior in Whom they believed had been born of this same people whose children they were now giving refuge, whose *flock doomed to slaughter*[36] they were now saving. The Lord knew clearly where He had led Buzya and Fishl, who had fled 2 kilometers and not knocked on a single door. The Sanevich family was the only family of believers on this street, and the Lord had led them straight there. Anna and Ivan knew the words of Jesus, who said: *He who receives whomever I send receives Me; and he who receives Me receives Him who sent Me.*[37] They knew His warning: *Assuredly, I say to you, inasmuch as you did it to one of the least of these My brethren, you did it to Me.*[38] That is what Anna told them: "Children, it's God who brought you directly to us; if you had gone into the house before us, a warden lives there, and in the house after us, a *polizei.*" "Having heard this," recalls Buzya, "I realized what a miracle the Lord had done for us. I looked at the calendar that hung on the wall: 31 October. I will remember that day my entire life." And all of the subsequent years of her long life, Buzya-Anna always spent that day in tears and prayer, and when possible, in fasting: the day that she lost all, and having lost all, was saved by Him. *I waited patiently for the Lord; and He inclined to me, and heard my cry. He also brought me up out of a horrible pit, out of the miry clay, and set my feet upon a rock, and established my steps.*[39]

"When we came in, I looked around the house: If the people were talking about God here, why were there no icons and images? But on the wall hung only a text from the Gospels: *The time is fulfilled, and the kingdom of God is at hand. Repent, and believe in the gospel.*[40] It was the first time in my life I had read those words, but how they touched my heart! And somehow I immediately decided that the people guided by such words could be trusted, and I opened my heart up to them, telling them all: Who we were, and from where, and how we came to them, and that our parents had just now been led out to be shot."

Interestingly enough, Fishl recalls a different verse. Apparently, both hung on the wall, but each was touched by something of his own. *God is love*[41] – like a healing balm, easing and anointing the wounds, these words poured into the boy's wounded heart. "I realized that we had found ourselves with good people. I could no longer hold back, and all the tension, all the torment, all the exhaustion of the past hours suddenly overcame me, and I fell to the floor and began to cry out: God, our God!"

Buzya and Fishl wept, telling their terrible story, and their hosts wept along with them, staggered by all they were hearing. When the children had finished their story, the Saneviches, naturally, went about setting up the brother and sister in their home, as if they were normal guests. The question didn't even arise of whether they should lodge there; it was as if, by making the decision to keep the Jewish children in their home, they weren't risking the lives of their own children. These scant remembrances I have read are comparable, in some sense, to a biblical account: They describe only the actions. There is not a word about what Anna and Ivan Sanevich must have been feeling when they made this tough decision – feelings that must have unsettled their hearts when they realized the danger they were subjecting their own children to from that moment on. I reread the recollections and think that for Buzya and Fishl, it must have been an incredible testimony of faith and closeness to God: God has to be absolutely real to you for you to be prepared to sacrifice what is most precious to you for His sake. In the *Aqedat Yitzhaq*, the story of Isaac's sacrifice, the first thing that astounds the reader is just how real, how close the Lord was in Abraham's life: God's voice was so clear and distinct for him, so distinct from any other voice, that despite the fact that His words differed this time from everything that God had told him before, not once did Abraham doubt whether God had given him this terrible command. *For he endured as seeing Him who is invisible.*[42] I never met either Anna, or Ivan – they died many years ago, and I don't know very much about them; but just as, in reading about the sacrifice of Isaac, one can deduce that Abraham knew and loved God, otherwise he simply could not have done what he did, in exactly the same way, by the very story that we are now in the midst of, one can see that they also knew and loved God, that they also lived *as seeing Him who is invisible*. After all, only by *seeing Him who is invisible* can we endure in the face of the most terrible of visible circumstances. Only by *seeing Him who is invisible* can we do what they did. Only for the One Who is absolutely real and infinitely loving can one sacrifice what is most precious.

"We were placed above the oven and covered with a curtain." In eastern Europe, the very large farm-style oven is the center of the home, much larger than its western analogues, sometimes rising up to the ceiling and heating the whole house via radiators. Above such an oven, there was always a loft, the coziest, warmest place in the house, big enough for people to sleep there. "Our clothes were not only washed, but also disinfected in the oven. They wanted to shave both of us bald, fearing lice, but the Sanevich sisters felt bad to shave off such 'beautiful curls,' as they called them, and one of them sat with me for several days, picking lice and nits out of my hair. For days on end, the youngest kept watch in the courtyard, warning us if anyone appeared near the house. At the slightest danger, we would immediately hide above the oven and be covered with a curtain."

"Frequently, Anna, the mother and mistress, would sit us down to the table and read aloud from God's Word. She told us about how Jesus Christ was that very Messiah of Israel whom the Jewish people had been waiting for all these centuries, and was still waiting for. Listening to her and reading the Gospel, I gradually began to understand that Jesus Christ was not 'the Gentile

God,' as I had thought my whole life, but that He was 'the Jewish God,' and that the Gospel had been written by Jews for Jews, and that it concerned Jews, including me, personally. So many generations in my family had waited for the *Mashiach,* the Messiah, and suddenly I had learned the truth: that He had already come, that He is, and that I can pray to Him."

In the second chapter, we spoke about the sealed book from Isaiah – a book containing חזות הכול – the whole vision – a book that is given to the *literate,* but he cannot read it because it is sealed. We also spoke about how we see the unsealing of this scroll, this plan of God, this חזות הכול – whole vision – in Chapter 5 of Revelation. In that chapter, there is a surprising scene – one that is very unexpected and full of the deepest prophetic meaning. John, who is weeping over the book, is told: "*Do not weep. Behold, the Lion of the tribe of Judah, the Root of David, has prevailed to open the scroll and to loose its seven seals.*"[43] Hearing this, he turns around, expecting to see the victorious Lion, and suddenly, instead of a Lion, he sees *a Lamb as though it had been slain.*[44] Can you imagine? You're expecting to see a Lion: strong, powerful, and victorious. But instead of a Lion, you see a Lamb: meek, innocent, helpless, and *as though it had been slain,* at that. This is such an incredible substitution that only He who possesses power could have performed it – and consequently, not flesh and blood, but only the Father in heaven can reveal and confirm it. When you are expecting a Lion, but a Lamb shows up instead, only God

Himself can confirm to you that this Lamb was sent by Him, and that it is the Lion. None of the other peoples were *literate,* so they weren't expecting a Lion. When a Lamb came, they loved and accepted Him as the Lamb. Israel, however, who is *literate,* was expecting a Lion from the tribe of Judah[45] – and though since the time in Egypt, Israel had always known about the lamb, about how the blood of the lamb saves and redeems, a special, incredible revelation from God was necessary for them to understand and accept that the Lion had become a Lamb. When the Lamb came, Israel needed a special revelation from God about how it was Him. That the meek Lamb was the mighty Lion. This is exactly what Yeshua is saying, in speaking to Peter: "*Blessed are you, Simon Bar-Jonah, for flesh and blood has not revealed this to you, but My Father who is in heaven.*"[46] This is that very removing of the seals, without which it is impossible to see and read the scroll. As long as the book is sealed, it is hidden; but when God Himself removes the seal, then the marvel happens that happened with Rabbi Shaul after the meeting on the road to Damascus: *Then you will know that the Lord of hosts has sent Me to you.*[47]

The same thing happened with Buzya and Fishl. Until now, having grown up in a Jewish family and having been instructed in the faith of Israel, they were in that sense *literate* – just as all of Israel, which is awaiting the Lion: the kingly Lion from the tribe of Judah, the Lion of the house of David, the Lion full of strength and majesty, the Lion that can crush and defeat, the Lion whose strong right arm will liberate His people from their enemies and *break the arm of the wicked and the evil man.*[48] But now, after everything that they had experienced, who, if not the ones *as though slain,* should recognize and accept the **Lamb as though it had been slain?** The darkness that had seemed impenetrable dissipated. The One Who had seemed somewhere very far away, strong and inaccessible, Who had allowed their sufferings and for some reason had not intervened, turned out to have borne all their sufferings together with them. *A Man of sorrows and acquainted with grief.*[49] Yeshua unsealed His Book before them – and light from above engulfed the tormented souls: a light of hope, a light of life and love. "It was that light," remembers Anna, "that had also shone into the soul of my mama in 1937, when the believers had come to visit her from the neighboring village, and she came to believe that Jesus is the Messiah of Israel. Later, Satan succeeded in changing her mind and stealing her from God; but we, by the grace of God, stood fast in the faith. From that moment, our path was only with Him – and from that day until now, He still leads us, and we seek His face always and everywhere. At that terrible moment of our lives, when we, having come to our senses after the initial fear and shock, aware that we had lost everything and everyone despite our physical lives being spared, when as a 16-year-old girl my head was full of gray hair, when our hearts were bursting from sorrow and bitterness, and when it was more than we could bear – it was at that very moment, in the darkness of our pain and hopeless situation, that we heard His quiet voice: *'And lo, I am with you always, even to the end of the age.'*[50] He became my Shepherd, my Teacher, my Friend – my God."

We know that during the time of the Holocaust, there were numerous such stories when Christians (not nominal, but true believers in Jesus) saved and hid Jewish children in their homes, and as a result, these children also "converted to Christianity." Why? Were they guided by the desire to be like their rescuers? Did they feel it necessary to assimilate into their surroundings and the people around them? Was it ordinary childish conformism? I am deeply convinced of what was already said in Chapter 1, which I want to reiterate here: Behind the visible façade of the numerous stories of the "conversion" of Jewish children to Christianity hides the great mystery of the unsealed Book and the Messiah of Israel who appears to His people – Who reveals Himself! When these Jewish children, *despised and rejected by men,* those from whom people *hid, as it were, their faces,* found out about the One Who was *despised and rejected by men,* about the One from Whom so many people *hid their faces,*[51] but Who, in this lowliness and disparagement, had overcome death – in amazement, joy, and gratefulness, they bowed before Him and gave Him their lives. Over and over again: Themselves *as if slain,* these Jewish children recognized and accepted the **Lamb as though it had been slain.** It was not meeting with Christian rescuers, no matter how full of light and love they were, but meeting the One Who Himself is Light and Love that forever changed the life of everyone who came out of the Holocaust believing in Yeshua. As Fishl wrote in his remembrances, citing many prophecies about Yeshua from the *Tanakh* and summarizing them (I read this only after I had already written everything that I have here): "I wrote about this, so that people could understand that I believed through the *Tanakh* – not through a person, no matter how good those people were who helped us."

Buzya and Fishl lived with the Saneviches for two months. It was clear to both the hosts and the children themselves that this situation could not continue indefinitely, that sooner or later they would be tracked down and therefore needed to leave. One evening, their hostess Anna, upon returning home, said: "I am making you Ukrainian passports – German *Ausweiskarten* – so that you can live freely as Ukrainians. You need only go away from here, over 100 kilometers, and no one will recognize you. Here is your new autobiography: "Your mother died; your father remarried and took a stepmother who was mean and bad, who offended you, so you decided to go somewhere away from your home, to set yourselves up somewhere to work." Then she asked the Schmiegers: "What first and last names will you take? Listen to my advice – you should take different last names on your passports, so people don't know you are brother and sister." She gently explained to Buzya that Fishl's Jewishness was very easily discerned: He was circumcised, which was dangerous for him, and would also be dangerous for her, if people found out that she was his sister. "That way at least you will survive." But Buzya responded: "I don't want to live without him. We will have the same last name and the same fate."

"The last name we chose for ourselves was Ilchuk (we purposefully chose it to start with the letter 'I' – to never forget that we are *Iudey,* or Jews); the first name I took was also that of our rescuer, Anna, so that I would never forget the good deed that she had done for us; and I took the patronymic Moiseyevna, again so as never to forget to which people I belong. My brother took the name Dmitry, with the same patronymic and last name as I took, of course. Literally within a few days, our passports were ready."

"Clean, well-fed, having eaten our full and grown strong following the terrible months at the ghetto, we were prepared to set out on our journey. But before saying our final farewells to the Saneviches, we decided to go back to our village, to Velikaya Volitsa, to collect some clothes that I had hidden with acquaintances just in case, before we were taken from the village."

"We left at night, of course, so that no one could see us. We safely reached the village and knocked on the doors of those few homes where I had hidden clothes. Only Nina opened to us; all the rest – our former fellow villagers whom we had considered friends – drove us Jews away from their windows and threatened to call the police. But at Nina's house, we wept for the entire night, said our goodbyes, and early in the morning, before dawn, we left to go back to the Saneviches in Lyubar.

"The next day, we left the Saneviches. The hosts, as they were able, had gathered clothing for us, baked flatbread, and given us food to take with us, as much as we could – and with tears and prayers, saw us off on our journey. Which way to go? To the left? To the right? Where should we turn? No one could give us a hint of where to go, but the One Who is the way, truth, and life, the One Who gave us life and revealed the truth to us – He had already determined our path.

"My first decision was: 'Let's go to Jerusalem.' I knew that we needed to go south – eight years of straight A's in geography had not been for nothing. I understood that to get to Palestine, one had to go to Odessa, and from there, the Black Sea, then Turkey, and from there, Jerusalem was already within reach. So they took us out to the highway heading south. Darya, the second daughter, took us there and bid us farewell. And we set off on our way – to Jerusalem."

Their desires and dreams – the same dream that had once also warmed the heart of her mama and grandfather – were fulfilled only a half century later. Exactly 50 years after that cold December day of 1941, He who is the way brought Anna to Jerusalem. But for now, the 16-year-old girl, with a small pack on her shoulders, was only beginning that long journey of a half-century – a journey that would end in Jerusalem....

"My short, thin brother Fishl walking next to me was now Dmitry – the only person I had left in the whole world. It was he, when we escaped from the ghetto, who had essentially saved my life. When I realized that my parents were being led out to be shot, I had cried out, wailing: 'Mama, mama, I want to go to you, let's run back; I don't want to live without them.' He, a small boy, with authority coming over him out of the blue, blocked my path and also wailing, said: 'Sister, will it really be easier for mama to lie in her grave if you are lying next to her? Let's run; we'll trust God. If He wants to leave us alive, He will lead us to good people!' Then we trusted in God, and He was faithful, performing the miracle that led us to the house of the Saneviches and saving us. What awaited us now? I looked at my brother, my heart breaking from pity and fear; but I remembered the sign that the Lord had showed me in the ghetto – two stars not falling, but rising – and strengthened by this memory, I continued on my way."

When, from where we sit today, I look back at those two thin figures from long ago, making their way along the empty highway against the backdrop of a blue November sky, and at the same time so distinctly see God's hand directing them, so clearly understand that the Lord doesn't leave them along on this journey, even for an instant – *and the children of Israel went out with boldness*[52] – I ask myself the question: Was it just as clear and convincing for them at the time? After all, not only for Buzya and Fishl, but also for each of us, it is much easier to perceive His hand in retrospect, once the story of God's victory is complete – and it is much more difficult to believe that the Lord Himself is directing our story before it is finished, before the victory has been won, when the miracle has yet to take place, and when we are yet **in the midst** of this story. But this is exactly what the Lord expects from us – and this is what is called faith, *the evidence of things not seen*. Remember the story about Elisha and his servant from Chapter 6 of 2 Kings? Elisha and his servant found themselves surrounded by enemies, and the servant asked in desperation: *"Alas, my master! What shall we do?"* Elisha, however, not in the least concerned about the seemingly completely hopeless circumstances, responds to him with the famous phrase: *"Do not fear, for those who are with us are more than those who are with them."* And when, clearly puzzled by this riddle of an answer, the servant turns around in every direction, trying to find those who were with them, Elisha prays to the Lord for him: *"Lord, I pray, open his eyes that he may see."*[53] In response to this prayer, the Lord truly opens the eyes of the servant so he suddenly sees God's host that is fighting for them: horses and chariots of fire around Elisha. But what about Elisha himself? Did he see these horses and chariots of fire before the servant, without a particular touch from the Lord? Naturally, he knew that the Lord was fighting for him, because he was so inclined – but did he see this divine host the way his servant saw it? For some reason, for my whole life, I had thought that yes, of course he saw them. He was a

71

prophet, a seer, and indubitably, he could see more than his servant. For my whole life, I thought that specifically because he saw, he was so calm. But today, the Lord very clearly showed me that the story is not about the prophetic gifts that Elisha was certainly generously endowed with, but it is first and foremost a story about his faith. Elisha, the man of God, more than anything else, was a man of faith – and therefore, believing, he knew that the Lord could not forsake them, that the Lord had surrounded them with His chariots. That is why he prayed only for his servant: for the one who needed to see it in order to believe. Elisha didn't need to see, because he **knew**. *"Because you have seen Me, you have believed. Blessed are those who have not seen and yet have believed."*[54] It is fantastic when the Lord opens our eyes and shows us angels in heaven, or chariots of fire, or two stars rising into heaven; but the Lord wants us to be able to live by faith, the evidence of things not seen, even when our faith has nothing visible to rely on....

"We had gone several kilometers away from Lyubar, when suddenly we saw a man coming toward us on a horse. I immediately recognized him – not so long ago, he had been a friend of my father's. He had been in our home every week, always a welcome guest, and mama would spread the table for him.... All of this had been very recent, only a few months ago.... But was it that man? 'Where are you going, *Zhidy*?' he said, using the derogative term for Jews; that's what he called us now. 'To burn the bread? Go back to the

Germans.' My brother was overcome with tears, and began to cry and beg. I asked: 'Sir, don't do evil. Take everything we have, just let us go.' And he agreed. I took the sack from my shoulder, took the large wool shawl from my shoulders. I gave him everything – and he let us go.'

So they left those places where they had been born and grew up, where people might still be able to recognize them. They went to where no one knew them, no one could recognize or identify them – no one, except for the One, Who not only didn't take His eyes off them for an instant, but Who led them by the hand Himself that whole time. *The One Who sees me lives.*

Chapter 4

THE ONE WHO
SEES ME LIVES

And God heard the voice of the lad.
Then the angel of God called… out of heaven,
and said to her… Fear not,
for God has heard the voice of the lad
where he is…. So God was with the lad.
(Genesis 21:17-20)

I have written before about how the *Aqedat
Yitzhaq*, the story of the sacrifice of Isaac, contains
– among its many other enigmas – one more
mystery that our sages have long pointed out.
After everything that happened on Mount
Moriah, after the raised knife was stopped by the
voice from heaven, Genesis 22:19 states: *So
Abraham returned to his young men, and they rose
and went together to Beersheba; and Abraham dwelt at
Beersheba.* Isaac isn't mentioned there at all. Where
did he disappear to? What happened to him after
the *Aqedah*? Historically, this circumstance has
triggered numerous discourses and speculations,
which are laid out in a wide variety of works by
our sages and rabbis. Where did Isaac go?
Wouldn't it be right for us to expect, after the
trauma the son had experienced, for Abraham to

have been obsessive over him, showing him even greater love and concern? Especially since ultimately, Abraham himself (though not by his own will, but by God's) had one way or another caused him this trauma? Wouldn't it be right for us to expect a story about how the father and son, after undergoing their joint testing, would have returned home together to the worried sick Sarah? (Remember: Back in those days, there were no mobile phones, or even landlines, and until Abraham returned to Beersheba, Sarah could not have had the slightest idea as to what had transpired on Mount Moriah.) But we don't find anything of the sort here: no expressions of the family's emotions on the occasion, no description of a cheery unity between the jointly tested father and son. The Scriptures inform us only about Abraham's return. Isaac vanishes, and he next appears in God's Word only in Genesis 24, right before the meeting with Rebekah, his future wife. Why?

Without lingering over the discourses and explanations of man, let's try to analyze what God's Word is telling us. It says in the Scriptures that *now Isaac came from the way of Beer Lahai Roi.*[55] In the next chapter, we also see it mentioned that *Isaac dwelt at Beer Lahai Roi.*[56] For a person who doesn't know Hebrew, this name means nothing. But a person who knows how to read this place name in Hebrew will be astounded by its profound meaning: The Well of **The One Who Sees Me Lives** – that is how I would translate it. What does the surprising name of this well tell us? That even after the *Aqedah*, after what he had experienced on Mount Moriah, when Isaac appears to disappear for some time from both his family, as well as our field of vision, when no one could see Isaac or knew where he was, the Lord still saw him. There is no doubt that God had His Own reason and plan for Isaac's temporary absence: This was surely a time of very close relationship between Isaac and the Lord, a time when not his earthly father, but his Heavenly Father Himself restored him after the terrible shock he had gone through. But even that is not the most important thing for us right now. The special, intimate meaning of these words is that while Isaac disappeared from everyone else, **he did not disappear for God.** Though his parents could not see him (they were quite possibly very worried because of it), and though he is not visible to us, the Lord still saw him and knew everything about him: *The One Who Sees Me Lives.* And I know that it is not by accident that the Lord gave me specifically these words for the title of this book. When they left Lyubar, our protagonists seemed to disappear to the whole life that they had lived up until then – just as **Isaac disappears** after the knife on Mount Moriah is raised and stopped; but the Lord is the One Who sees and doesn't leave them for a moment. With His hand, He leads the brother and sister, with His hand he directs, protects, and preserves them, and with His hand He shepherds the sheep *doomed for slaughter....* And so it seems right to me that here, in this chapter, we mainly hear their voices – the voices of Buzya and Fishl. Just as no

one besides Isaac himself can testify about the
time when he lived at *Beer Lahai Roi*, in exactly the
same way, no one except they themselves can tell
about their life at that well: **The One Who Sees Me
Lives.** So, here are some excerpts from the
recollections of Buzya and Fishl, whom we came
to know and love here in Israel as Anna and
Dmitry (we learned their actual names much
later, from their writings).

***

Anna: "It grew terribly cold outside. After giving
away my shawl, I felt this cold literally every
second, in every cell of my chilled-to-the-bone
body. It was extremely hard to keep walking. We
walked the whole day, and we entered the village
of Krasnopol to stay the night. Before entering the
village, we tested each other once again, to see
whether we knew our 'autobiography' well: It
turned out that we both knew it by heart, that we
were Anna and Dmitry Ilchuk, and where we had
come from.

"We stayed overnight with some people whose
only son, a 20-year-old, had just died a few weeks
before. They were very happy to have us and
began advising us to stay in their village: It's too
cold already, they said, to go further, and we
would be able to find work here if our documents
were in order. I heeded their advice. We stayed in
their home, and for the entire winter, I worked at
the village's silo, where the grain was stored.
Before that, the warden checked my documents,
said everything was in order, and sent me to the
silo. As a 16-year-old, the labor was back-

breaking for me: I was supposed to carry heavy, scarcely liftable sacks; but I was very happy to have even this work. My brother worked at the house and also collected and dried fuel, so it was warm in the house from the fire and the smoke.

"How did we live, how did we survive that first winter? At the communal farm where I had gotten the work, they allotted me 16 kilograms of wheat and 16 kilograms of peas for the month. Per month, this worked out to approximately a pound for the both of us per day – half a pound each. The grain had to be milled, made into flour, and then baked into bread or pancakes. Once, I had this happen to me: I mixed up the dough for the pancakes and set it in a warm place to rise in the great oven; but there in the oven, our hostess also happened to be warming some chicks that had just hatched – she had put them in the warm oven so they could dry out and warm up. When the dough rose, I went to mix it again and noticed that there was some sort of glob that would not mix in. When I finally managed to stir it in, it turned out to have been a chick that had somehow gotten into the pail with the dough and had drowned in it. Of course, after that, I was unable to touch a thing and didn't eat those pancakes, and so went hungry the whole day.

"Every day brought ever new difficulties; there is not enough paper to describe all the trials and tribulations. How did we survive it all? Who gave us strength to endure and keep going, to bear all the sorrows and trials and even rejoice in the midst of these sufferings? As the Apostle Paul writes, *I can do all things through Messiah who strengthens me.*[57] That same Lord and Messiah Who had been revealed to us at the Sanevich's home did not leave us and preserved our hearts in peace.

"Having settled in Krasnopol, I began to look for the same type of believers as the Saneviches. I started asking around, at first unsuccessfully, but then finally, someone said: Yes, there are several people here who are very strange. They call themselves believers, but they have no crosses, nor images; they are totally different. They don't light candles, don't pray to the icons; we have nothing in common with them. They were also called 'stundists.' How I rejoiced at this news and immediately went to the address they had indicated – and truly, found a gathering of Evangelical believers. I began attending their gatherings regularly, on Wednesdays and Sundays. There were only a few people, no more than eight, and sometimes no more than three or four sisters who gathered. But I can still feel that joy, peace, and blessing today that I received there, praying together with those three or four sisters. God's Word, which was spoken there, concerned me directly – and my Jewish people.

"Soon, I came to trust the sisters and revealed to them who we were and from where. This didn't change their attitude toward me. The same love, the love of the Lord, shined in them. I ran home happy, transformed, and told all to my brother. He received the Word of Life from me. He himself tried to go out in public as little as possible – his outward appearance was too Jewish. I also looked Jewish, of course, but not as strongly, and by covering my curly hair with a white scarf, I was not afraid to go outside and let people see me. Incidentally, in a surprising way, Anna Sanevich had seen to everything – truly, God's Spirit had directed her – and, led by the love of the Lord and His wisdom, she had chosen for us a 'birthplace' that totally justified our outward appearance. In our passports, it was written that we had been born in the Gvozdyansk District of the Romanov Region – and people born in that region were known for being dark-skinned."

And now, summer had arrived – the first summer after that long, terrible winter. A winter in which they had lost everything – and having lost all, obtained God. In Anna's recollections of a later time, the years of 1944-1945, there are so many tears, so much pain and longing for their loved ones. But when I read and reread the pages about Krasnopol and find there barely a word about these parents who had been killed only a few months prior, I clearly understand that during these first months, the Lord had protected them not only physically. The Heavenly Father, doctor, and healer, by filling their hears with the *peace of God, which surpasses all understanding,*[58] preserved their souls Himself from attacks of the maddening, piercing, unbearable pain of loss with His own spiritual anesthesia (and this divine drug persisted until this pain was no longer so great as to be unbearable in their own power). "God was the most important thing in our life," remembers

Anna. "The Lord taught us to place all our cares on Him, and in everything, literally everything, we saw His hand. I began to go to gatherings in other villages, as well, sometimes going 10-15 kilometers to get to a service. I especially wanted to go to the meetings where there were young people. Upon returning, I would come to my sisters in Krasnopol, bringing them heartfelt greetings from the brothers and sisters in the faith. It was as if I had a family again – I came to love all the brothers and sisters, as if I had gained a large kinsfolk. The loneliness faded.

"That same summer, it was announced at all the churches that there would be a teaching on baptism. I had dreamed about this covenant with the Lord since I had come to know and love the Messiah. Soon, the day was set, as well as the place of the baptism: the village of Kolodyazhno, in Polonsky Region. From Krasnopol, where I was, I had to pass through the Lyubar Region, and then I would reach Kolodyazhno. The same River Sluch on whose banks our ghetto had stood not so long ago flowed through there. It was also in the Sluch that we received baptism – God's promise for a clean conscience. We committed to be faithful to Him and to His word. There was nothing to ride in; we had to walk. We could not make it in a day; we were forced to stop somewhere for the night. I stayed with people who were recommended by one of the brethren who had supported me greatly spiritually. All the believers in the region knew who we were and knew about our origins. I was not afraid of the brothers and sisters – I considered them all people of God, the same as the Saneviches, and dreamed of becoming like them myself. I prayed about this and walked a long way to enter into a covenant with Him.

"The Lord was with me and led me Himself by His plan. Even today, I clearly remember that day: Over 50 people lined up near the river in white clothing. I also stood there in white clothing, though I don't remember who had lent it to me. The presbyter, Brother Adam, passed down the rows. I remember how he laid his hand on my head like a father. I know that it was a blessing and touch from the Savior. Even today – now I am 80, and then I was 16 – I remember this sweet touch of a fatherly hand, filling my heart with lightness and joy.

"After the baptism, I attended my Krasnopol church has a full-fledged member. I continued to read God's Word and various spiritual literature, which greatly touched my heart, and the New Testament was opened up to me. I sought only one thing: to be closer to Him: *One thing I have desired of the Lord, that will I seek: That I may dwell in the house of the Lord All the days of my life, to behold the beauty of the Lord, and to inquire in His temple.*[59]

"Of course, we did have trials and temptations; there were situations that we could not have gotten through if His hand had not preserved us. Once, I came home after a gathering in the neighboring village. The neighbors met me and said: Anna, your father waited here the whole day for you, crying, and saying: I know I'm to blame, that my second wife offended my children, and that's why they left. He was carrying clay pots to sell and came here to escort his children home, but his horse grew ill, and he couldn't wait; he had to leave. He asked to tell you that he was sorry, and asked you to come home, that now, everything would be different.

"Not long before that, I had started to hear rumors that there were 'well-wishers' in the village who had taken an interest in us, saying: Aren't those children Jewish? They really look like Jews! And then – was it not a miracle of God? – God sent us a 'father,' confirming all of our stories. The most astounding thing was that he had been exactly from those places where, according to our passports, my brother and I were from. What could we say? We could only thank God! Now, everyone in the village was convinced that we had a father, that he was really looking for us and waiting for us, and people told me: 'Anna, go home, don't be offended at your father,' and I responded: 'Never, my stepmom beat me so hard,' and I teared up – in truth, I had many reasons for tears.

"In 1942, the youth from Ukraine had started to be gathered to Germany, for forced labor. Since according to my documents, I was Ukrainian, they were supposed to come and take me, too. I was afraid to go to Germany, but even more afraid to leave Fishl, knowing that he bore the sign of circumcision, and I realized just how much the danger would grow if he were to be left alone. I prayed and went to the German superintendent of the region, asking for them not to take me, saying that we were orphans, and I could not leave my brother. I had to walk 20 kilometers. When I still had another 5 kilometers or so to go, I passed a cemetery, and a large black cat ran out of the cemetery and crossed the road in front of me. The rest of the way, I walked in tears: 'A black cat ran across the road; that means the trip will be a failure, not a success.' Surprisingly, God spoke to me even through this: The Lord taught me to trust Him alone, and not empty superstitions. I remembered this lesson my whole life: Despite the 'bad omen,' the superintendent welcomed me very warmly (not suspecting, of course, that a Jewish girl was before him). He wrote a note to the warden so that I wouldn't be touched, since I had a young orphan brother – and for some time, I was truly left alone. We both calmed down a little; it seemed that now, everything would work out. But time passed, and all the young people had been taken from the village, yet the Germans continued to demand people – and so then I was also ordered to go to the departure point, to be sent to Germany.

"How heavy my heart was! Can you imagine how it was for me, a Jewish girl, to think I would find myself in Germany, not to mention how difficult and frightening it was for me to leave my brother? But there was nothing I could do: I gave my brother my boots, my sweater, said goodbye, and left. I could not imagine what sort of future awaited me and my brother. I really hoped that the believing sisters would take care of him. But my main comfort was that I knew for certain: My brother was in God's hands, and the Lord would not leave him."

***

Dmitry: "Anna was very close and open with the believers, while I did not speak openly with anyone; I could not tell the truth about us. Once, Anna came home and said: 'Dmitry, I told Anna Bugovarova the whole truth about us, who we are and from where. Now she knows that we are Jews.' It wasn't that I had anything against Anna Bugovarova, but it seemed to me that it would be better if no one knew anything about us. Sometime after my Anna had been taken to Germany, and I had nowhere to live, nowhere to go, because I knew almost no one in the village, I was forced to ask Anna Bugovarova if I could stay with her, and then she, knowing that I was Jewish and fearing for her own children (she had a grown son and daughter, both medics), refused me. I thought that if Anna would not have told her that we were Jews, she would have agreed to take me in. So, for me, in my human reasoning, there was no hope left.

"I left the home of the Bugovarovs, sat under the windows, and began to cry. I cried for a long time – several hours – crying as long as the tears came, but no one except the Almighty saw these tears. But He not only saw, He answered these tears. Within a few days, I was thanking God for His miraculous answer to my tears and my prayer: I was charged with pasturing two cows, one belonging to a woodsman, and one to a family with the last name of Menchinsky. I would sleep at the Menchinsky home, have lunch at the woodsman's, where I was well fed until I was full, and the rest of the time, I grazed the cows in the forest. There, in the forest, I was completely alone. Fearing no one, I could sing, cry, and pray. For hours, I would pour out my heart before God there. Now that Anna had left, and I was completely alone, He was my only rock and protection."

Anna: "When I left, my brother was totally alone. It was very difficult for the believing sisters in Krasnopol: They knew that they could not abandon my brother, and that they truly needed to take care of him, but how could they do it? Knowing that my brother was Jewish, they were afraid to take him in, fearing for their own children. Finally, they found a way: In the forest lived a woodsman, and he agreed to take my brother on as a shepherd. My brother grazed his cow, along with another cow – it helped the owners. In the forest, the boy had time to cry out all his pain and grief before the Lord, and always and in everything, God was with him. During the long autumn evenings, the woodsman would call the boy in to himself to listen to his stories about God and the Bible. My brother knew a lot about the Bible, and gradually the woodsman came to the conclusion that a Ukrainian boy could not have such knowledge. Who was he? The woodsman wondered, and suspicions were sown in his heart. Rumors were circulating, and at some point, other shepherds of approximately his age decided to 'bare the mystery.' Four boys got together, and in the evening, they fell on Dmitry, threw him to the ground, pulled down his pants, and thus uncovered the secret that, in fact, meant a death sentence for him. This, it would seem, should have been the end of the life and story of my brother, Dmitry-Fishl, but in a completely astounding way, this secret that had been discovered somehow remained a secret. How and why? Did these boys take pity on him? Was it by order of the woodsman who was interested in keeping his shepherd? I don't know how to explain this enigma with human reasoning, but I know its true meaning: Those two stars that the Lord showed me back in the ghetto – those two stars that despite every physical law did not fall, but rose into heaven – those two stars were still in His hands. Miraculously, despite every physical and human law, He was directing us in His paths."

Dmitry: "As long as I was shepherding the cows of the Menchinsky family and the woodsman, I was taken care of, but the time came when the Menchinsky cow was taken from them, and they no longer needed my help. So I once again found myself without a roof over my head, since I had been sleeping in their home all this time. But the Lord was faithful: I was taken in by an elderly woman with the last name of Kucheryavaya. This woman, a believer, lived at the very edge of Krasnopol together with her unbelieving husband and did not enjoy particular respect in the village – and yet, she turned out to be the one through whom the Lord helped me. This happens frequently: Those who are despised and rejected by other people turn out to be the most open to God about helping others. In the Book of Joshua, the Bible tells about how Rahab the harlot hid the Israelites in her home when they came to spy out Jericho, and she received a great reward for this later, when the Israelites took the city: Not only her life, but the lives of her whole household were spared. I think that if Anna Bugovarova would have agreed to take me in, she would also have had a reward from the Lord – but this reward ended up going to Kucheryavaya.

"So, now I lived at Mrs. Kucheryavaya's house, and at least I had a constant roof over my head. But my life was still full of dangers and trials. For example, once when I was working, some Germans appeared. They came right up to me and began speaking in German. I knew German, I understood what they were saying, but seeing them made me feel so faint that I could hardly stand on my feet. It was with difficulty that I was able to say a few words, apologizing, saying that I had to go take care of my personal needs, and I left. When I returned, they were gone. Only someone who has experienced such a thing can understand how I felt at that moment, seeing that they had left.

"Anna was already a convinced and confirmed believer in Jesus; she had accepted baptism, she went to the meetings, and frequently retold me what she had heard there. As for me, back at the Saneviches, when Anna had read God's Word to us, my heart had burned. Essentially, I also came to believe back at the Saneviches. But, unlike Anna, I had still been unable to make a final decision: Could I, a Jew, believe in Jesus? Wasn't that betraying my relationship to my people? Was Jesus really that same Messiah of Israel about which our prophets had prophesied and whom my people were waiting for? When Anna left, I realized that the time had come for me to make a decision, as well. At Mrs. Kucheryavaya's house, there was an old, pre-Revolution edition of the Bible, and I undertook to read it, with the firm intention of finding out the truth and making the decision that God was expecting from me. I want to share just a few of the passages from the Bible that so clearly spoke to my heart at that time.

"In Genesis Chapter 3, after the fall into sin, God says when speaking to the serpent: *And I will put enmity between you and the woman, and between your seed and her Seed; He shall bruise your head, and you shall bruise His heel.*[60] Suddenly, I clearly understood that specifically this prophecy had been fulfilled at Golgotha.

"The Lord promises Abraham repeatedly: *Abraham shall surely become a great and mighty nation, and all the nations of the earth shall be blessed in him.*[61] The Messiah Jesus was an Israelite, a Jew, the descendant of Abraham, but He had opened the way to the God of Israel for all other peoples. Everyone who believes in Yeshua, no matter to which people he belongs, will be saved and called the son of Abraham.

"When blessing his sons before his death, Jacob-Israel says about Judah: *The scepter shall not depart from Judah, nor a lawgiver from between his feet, until Shiloh comes; and to Him shall be the obedience of the people.*[62] It would seem that specifically Joseph should have received such a blessing: As the most beloved of all of Jacob's sons and besides being the only one who had truly been elevated by the Lord, he was the only one of the brothers whose descendants might have been imagined at that moment with a scepter. But Jacob blesses not Joseph, but Judah with these words – and the prophetic meaning of this blessing is revealed gradually, when at first, King David from the tribe of Judah came to the throne of Israel, and then the Messiah, the Son of David, also came from this same tribe.

"The promise in the *Tanakh* about the New Covenant was very important for me; it became the final confirmation that my decision was right: *'Behold, the days are coming, says the Lord, when I will make a new covenant with the house of Israel and with the house of Judah – not according to the covenant that I made with their fathers in the day that I took them by the hand to lead them out of the land of Egypt, My covenant which they broke, though I was a husband to them, says the Lord. But this is the covenant that I will make with the house of Israel after those days, says the Lord: I will put My law in their minds, and write it on their hearts; and I will be their God, and they shall be My people.'*[63]

"I could share many other passages from the Bible, but I have written out just a few of these verses so that those who read my testimony can know: No matter how wonderful the believers in Jesus were whom the Lord sent across our path, I came to believe in Jesus based on the Word of God, through the *Tanakh*, and not through people. As Yeshua Himself says: '*Search the Scriptures, for… these are they which testify of Me.*'[64] I searched the Scriptures and accepted their testimony; and from that moment, I firmly knew that Jesus is that Messiah of Israel and that I, specifically as a Jew, should believe in my Messiah."

***

Anna: "So, I arrived in Germany. We were brought there in cargo wagons, together with many other young Ukrainians from various places. They barely fed us along the way; they gave us some sort of broth with potato peelings. Many could not handle it and tried to run away. Panic, tears. I was waiting for the end.

"The first thing that they did to us in Berlin was to take our fingerprints. Then, farmers, our future masters, began to come up to us. They examined us, looked us over, but most importantly, they checked the muscles of our arms. Which of us would make a good laborer? A diminutive German about 50 years old came up to me, looked in the eyes of this tall, thin girl in a white kerchief (I never parted from this kerchief all five years of the war) – and began to process the documents to procure himself a laborer – 'Ostarbeiter,' or Eastern Workers, as we were called in Germany.

"He was from the village of Shaksdorf, 20 kilometers from Berlin. After he had processed my documents, we walked on foot to his village, all 20 kilometers. I still remember the piece of bread that he gave me to eat before our journey. All that time, since the beginning of the war, I had not eaten home-baked bread. If we happened to have a handful of flour, we had baked pancakes or flatbread, to economize. But this was genuine, fresh, homemade bread. In my life, I have never tasted bread more delicious than that. He gave me two pieces, each the entire width of the loaf, generously spread with butter. This was his 'zweites Frühstück'. Later, I learned that between breakfast and lunch, my master always had a snack; there, on the road from Berlin, he had given me this snack, taking pity on the undernourished girl.

"He had not been mistaken in his choice of me, and all that time I was in his house, to the very end of the war, I served him just like the Apostle Paul calls on us to serve masters – *as to the Lord, and not to men*.[65] His house was split into two homes: In one, he lived with his wife, and his sister lived in the neighboring one. His name was Reinhart Linke, his sister Bata Linke. She was unmarried, very beautiful, with a long golden braid that she wrapped around her head. When my master and I arrived, he called Bata over, acquainted us, and told me: You will live with her, in her half. Both of us rejoiced, since from the very beginning, we really liked each other.

"Every day, I spent all of my free time with her. She came to trust in me, and I did, too. At first, my Yiddish really helped me; besides that, starting from fourth grade, I had studied German in school, and now my excellent grades really came in handy. Within three months, I was speaking German fluently. The masters, of course, did not know that I was Jewish, but in everything else I was completely open with them, especially with Bata. Bata and I spoke about everything. I once asked her how she viewed what Hitler was doing to the Jews. She answered me: Is Hitler really the leader of Germany? Here is our leader. And closing the shutters, she got out from some shelf a large portrait of the Kaiser and his family – his wife and children – and began to tell me about his merits, about how his wife had visited orphanages and hospitals and had donated much to the poor. 'Hitler is a disgrace to the German people; we are simply ashamed of him,' said Bata. 'Especially what he has done to the Jews, people who have given Germany such culture and have so enriched our country.' It was so pleasant for me to hear this. How happy I was that I had ended up with such excellent masters; after all, the phrases I had heard from the *polizei* in the ghetto still rang in my ears: 'No matter; soon it will be nearly impossible to find a single one of you Jews; you will all be defeated.' (In Lyubar, that is truly what happened: Of the 7,000 Jews of Lyubar, only my brother and I were left, and one other youth who had miraculously survived.)

"The Linke farm was large: 20 hectares of land, 20 hectares of forest, a horse, cows, pigs, and sheep. The mistress was ill, and so the master and I bore the burden of this whole farm. A large amount of what it produced was subject to very strict controls and given to the state, and it was for this reason that a laborer – an Ostarbeiter – had been given to him to help him with the farming. I helped my master, and the Lord helped me, and therefore, the master treated me very well.

"Bata cared for me like a mother. In the evenings, I would fall into bed, with no feeling in my hands or feet, since the work was still very difficult, and often, after I had already laid down to sleep, she would come into my bedroom to fluff up the feather bed or correct my blanket. She not only gave me her clothes, but also had her tailor to adjust them for me. That way, I did not need the clothes that the German officials gave out to Ostarbeiteren.

"Once, the order was given that the German masters were not to eat together with the laborers, but were to feed them where the livestock were fed. When he heard that, my master flew into an inconsolable rage: 'What do you mean – work together, and eat separately?' He did not heed this law a single day: From the very first day in their home, I ate at the same table with them."

Dmitry: "For some time, I stayed in Krasnopol and lived at Mrs. Kucheryavaya's, and then I went on further, from village to village. I got to the village of Kovalyenok, and there, one woman invited me to work for her, to shepherd her cow while she was busy sowing. I worked for her until the planting season was over; then, I once again set out on my way.

"I no longer remember the names of all the villages through which I passed. In some places, I shepherded cows; in some places, I worked on communal farms. Finally, I reached Lyubar, and there, in the city, I began to look around and think about where I could live. I remembered that at the market, I had seen a woman selling salt. I asked her: How much does salt cost? She answered me: 15 rubles a cup. And where do you get it? I asked her. She replied: in Kolomensk. I rejoiced, deciding that I could also live on that, and went to Kolomensk to buy salt. I bought as much as I could carry, came to the station, and found the train going to Shepetovka. But when the train came, I realized that I would not be able to drag the sack of salt into the wagon. What was I to do? But even there, the Lord did not forsake me. I saw that some roguish-looking guys were sitting on the roof of the train, older and stronger than me – and, since I had no choice, I asked them to help me carry the salt into the wagon. Surprisingly enough, they not only helped me carry the sack, but also guarded me and my load all the way to Shepetovka.

"So, I got from Kolomensk to Shepetovka, a distance of at least 700 kilometers, which took approximately 12 hours. Then, from Shepetovka, I could get to Peschanovka on any train, and from there, I worked to get on the cargo train going to Lyubar, and eventually I got all the way to

Lyubar. In Lyubar, I gave the salt to the woman, and she paid me immediately: She bought the salt from me for 10 rubles a cup, and sold it for 15, so it was very profitable for her. It was also very profitable for me, because I had bought the salt for 4 or 5 rubles a cup, and had sold it for 10. That way, I collected enough money to enter the eighth grade, because I really wanted to go to school. It was the 1944-1945 school year."

Anna: "In Germany, I sought out believers from the very beginning. Soon, I found a small group of sisters who lived in a barracks and worked at a factory, where they manufactured components for the front. They were fed turnips, mainly. They were constantly hungry, and their life was very difficult. I was happy to have the opportunity to help them. Every day, I put aside my Frühstück, my midmorning snack – those same two pieces of bread that my master had shared with me when we met. Yes, sometimes it was difficult to wait from breakfast at five in the morning to lunch at one o'clock in the afternoon, but then how delicious lunch seemed after such an interval! And on Sunday, when the sisters came, I had something to share with them: After six days, I had accumulated 12 pieces of bread.

"I continued to look for a congregation. Once, I attended an official German church – Lutheran – together with my Bata. There were many people there, but they all prayed for the leaders of the country, with some praying aloud, and the rest loudly saying 'Amen.' I didn't go there anymore; I had no desire to pray for a murderer. Soon, I found a small gathering of believers in the city of Finsterwald and began to attend regularly.

"The Almighty blessed me with good treatment from my masters and had made my life easier, but my tears had not dried up. After lunch, I would usually go out into the field and walk along the railroad tracks; the rails would be wet from my tears. I always remembered my father and mother; they were so beautiful and young; I thought about my five-year-old brother and my beautiful blue-eyed grandfather, who had been only 60 years old…. But even with such grief, God comforted me with His love. People around me seemed to sense my pain. The master and his wife once offered me: 'Anna, let us adopt you. The war will end; the army will come with our men; you can get married. I can will you all my possessions; you will be my daughter.' I said that I had a very dear brother, and I couldn't live without him. He responded that my brother could be sought and issued documents to come through the Red Cross. But I didn't agree to it, realizing that my brother had the sign of circumcision according to the laws of Moses on his body, and that they would immediately be able to tell that he was a Jew."

I am looking at Anna's photograph, taken there in Germany in 1944: An 18-year-old beauty with a classic Jewish face. Can you imagine: A completely Jewish girl, whose entire family is annihilated at a ghetto, lived for two years in the very heart of Hitler's Germany, 20 kilometers from Berlin. Is it not a miracle? I cannot find any other explanation for it but as a miracle, and eyes kept dim by the Lord Himself, just as the Lord had once closed the eyes of the *polizei* in the ghetto to save Buzya and her brother. Furthermore, the Lord was blessing not just Anna; he blessed the entire Linke home thanks to her: *The Lord blessed the Egyptian's house for Joseph's sake; and the blessing of the Lord was on all that he had in the house and in the field.*[66] And sensing this blessing, the masters themselves not only treated their young "Ukrainian" laborer completely differently, but also sought to understand what was so special about this laborer, what sort of unique secret was hidden within her, and what was the source of that blessing on her and their whole house.

"Once, when my masters came home in a very good mood after visiting their relatives, we sat down to eat at the common table, as always, and during lunch, the master said to me: 'Anna, you have been working for us for a rather long time now. I am always looking at you, and I have come to the conclusion that you are no Ukrainian.' Can you imagine what I felt in those minutes? I sat there, fiddling with my white scarf, while underneath the table, my poor knees were not only shaking, they were practically knocking together. That's it, I was thinking. They have found me out to be Jewish; my final hour has come. But he continued: 'After all, so many Germans were in Russia back 200 years ago, under Catherine the Great. Perhaps you simply don't know it, but it's likely that your father or grandfather is German, which means you are a real German!' It was as if a huge weight fell from my soul, since I was already preparing myself for a full 'reveal.' Encouraged, I answered the master: 'I know for certain that my mother is Ukrainian, but I'm not certain concerning my father. Perhaps you are right. Perhaps he was really a German.'"

***

Thus passed the days, weeks, and months – a whole two years. Everything, even the most terrible of times, comes to an end at some point, and the end of this terrible war had come, as well. "The Allies opened a second front. The entire sky over Berlin was ablaze with red, for the city was being bombed daily; we were waiting day to day to see whether we would be freed and sent back to Ukraine. My master didn't think that I planned to leave, and so soon; he had been hiding and burying everything he had, because the Germans had taken everything in the house. Among his things, he hid the presents I had accumulated from Bata – and so, when I was finally able to go home, I was left with nothing at all. I left in what I was wearing. I did find a couple precious items: a pillow and a large red flag, from which later I sewed myself a dress, after dying it black."

We have now reached the point in our narration where it is said: *Now Isaac came from the way of Beer Lahai Roi.*[67] Isaac returns to the pages of the Scriptures, to the family story, to the place where his life had been spent before Mount Moriah, where the knife had been raised over him – and he came from that place that is called *Lahai Roi*, the One Who Sees Me Lives, the place where no one saw him or knew of him except the Lord. In exactly the same way, Anna-Buzya, after an endless four years, returned to the place where she had spent her life before the knife had been raised, coming from the place where no one had known her except for the Lord – from the place where she had been invisible and inaccessible to anyone who knew and remembered her, but where the Lord unfailingly maintained His watch over her. *The One Who Sees Me Lives.*

Anna: "Upon arriving in Lyubar, I immediately went to the Saneviches, in hopes that they would know something about my brother. It turned out that yes, they knew, and that he was living in Lyubar. They informed him I had come, and he immediately ran to me: My Fishl, Mitya, my brother, the dearest person I had in the whole world! How he had grown during these years – how big, tall, and handsome he had become. He had a mustache growing; his hair had changed – a real man. It turned out that he not only had managed to complete some sort of trade school for processing topsoil, but he had even begun working, and several other people were already working under him."

Their grandfather's house in Lyubar had been completely destroyed by the bombings. Dmitry had rented an apartment in the city, and Anna also settled there for a time. Thanks to her good knowledge of mathematics, she was given a job as a bookkeeper – and so, the brother and sister began their post-war peacetime life. She would walk around Lyubar as if in a dream – once again, the city reveled in greenery; once again, the gardens were blossoming; once again, the Sluch glistened in the sun. How was it possible? Perhaps it had all been a terrible dream? But in this peaceful, blooming Lyubar, there were no longer mother and father and little brother, nor grandmother and grandfather, nor many of their friends whom they had known and remembered from childhood – the thousands of Jews shot in 1941 in the Peshchanoye district were missing. And though at the time, there was no memorial at the site of the atrocious murders – and would not be for a long time – the very absence of Lyubar's Jews had left a yawning hole, a gap. This void that they had left served more eloquently than any monument as a constant reminder of everything that had been here before: *The voice of your brother's blood cries out to Me from the ground.*[68] And how many vacant villages, towns, and cities there were all across Ukraine! And each of them with their own Peschanoye, their own Baby Yar: some gulley, pit, or former animal burial site where the *voice of blood* truly *cries out from the ground.*

Anna: "It was very difficult for me to live in Lyubar. They say that time heals. It's not true. My pain did not subside, and I was always remembering my mother, father, little brother, grandmother, and grandfather." The monastery on that bank of the Sluch – the former ghetto – was constantly before her eyes. And even when Anna managed to avoid it physically, her inner gaze, thoughts, and feelings were still focused there, on those autumn days of 1941. The terrible days of the ghetto, despite the suffering and horror of everything that was experienced there, became like a magnet for her memories, since those were the last, truly priceless days and hours with her parents, and she returned to them in her thoughts again and again.

She almost had not expected this, and was in no way prepared for it. Until then, Anna had always been occupied with her and her brother's physical survival. But now that their lives were no longer threatened for the first time in all these years, the longing and grief literally consumed her. The pain of returning for the first time in all those years to this place where all her loved ones had previously always been alongside her, the daily pain of eyes scorched by the sight of that terrible building – immovable, as if nothing had happened in that former orphanage overlooking the Sluch – this pain would engulf her, starting at her head, like a wave, and she would feel like she was drowning, being submerged, that she could not get to the surface for air. She suffered this agony many times a day and ultimately realized that sooner or later, she would have to leave Lyubar, that she could not go on living there.

Anna: "Of course, I really wanted to visit Nina, to thank her for everything she had done for us, and simply to see her, and that's the only reason I went to the village, to Velikaya Volitsa. Learning that I had returned, the entire village came running out to see their former fellow villagers – some to look at people 'risen from the dead,' some simply out of curiosity. There were also those who wanted to somehow 'comfort' me, to add to my sufferings. For example, one neighbor woman told me that after we had been taken away, our cat had run around the village, hysterically mewing and not letting anyone come near it – and thus, her meowing had been heard for nearly six months. Another neighbor woman shared the details that she had heard from her *polizei* husband: that there, in Peschanoye, where the Jews had been shot, my father had not been shot until the very end of the executions; he had been ordered to push those who were already dead into the pit and had been shot only at the end. I don't know why they told me all this; I am surprised that my heart could take it all in. Even to this day, it bleeds at the memory of it. I hurried to leave the village, so as to never return."

Meanwhile, legends had already sprung up concerning the things they had lived through and experienced, and about their miraculous salvation. "Once, I was riding in a truck with some friends – there were practically no buses, people moved about on trucks – and I heard one of the passengers tell the others the story of Fishl and myself – not suspecting that the very girl he was describing was sitting next to them. "Such a heroic destiny, this brother and sister, true heroes," finished his narration. I listened to his story, as if about someone else, and was shaken by the last phrase in surprise. We were heroes? Yes, many times my brother and I had stared death in the eyes, but I know that only by His strength, *we are more than conquerors through Him who loved us.*[69] We were able to live through all this and overcome. *"If it had not been the Lord who was on our side," let Israel now say – "If it had not been the Lord who was on our side, when men rose up against us..."*[70]

***

Like Isaac, the Lord blessed Anna with a long life. And though she would have to live in Ukraine for many, many more years, in the autumn of 1991, exactly 50 years after that day when two Jewish children left the home of the Saneviches to head to Jerusalem, the most important thing happened that she had been waiting for and preparing for her whole life: Anna Kiyanovskaya (Buzya Schmieger) made a*liyah* – immigrated to Israel – and came to Jerusalem. "There were many obstacles in my path: My only daughter did not want to go, so my only beloved granddaughter also had to stay in Ukraine. But, having consulted with my brothers in the faith, I double-checked and felt certain that the decision was not mine, that it was God's decision, God's plan, and on 10 October 1991, I left for Israel. I came to Jerusalem completely alone – all of my loved ones had stayed in Ukraine for the time being. I was 66 years old.

"How much joy I experienced when I stepped into the white-stoned Jerusalem. Everywhere, there were Jews; everywhere, there were signs in Hebrew (oh, these Hebrew letters, so dear to my heart, known to me since childhood). After all, I still remember the words of the *polizei* in the ghetto: 'Soon it will be nearly impossible to find a single one of you Jews; you will all be defeated.' How great is your mercy, Lord, how infinite Your faithfulness to Your people!"

Of course, Anna hoped that both her daughter and her family, as well as her brother would come with her to Israel, and that is what happened. That same year, her daughter requested that invitations be processed for her. Her brother and his wife came a little later. Her brother, Dmitry Schmieger, together with his wife Maria, live in Beersheba (that same place Isaac once returned to after coming up from *Beer Lahai Roi)*, along with the families of his children, who also came to Israel. Anna Kiyanovskaya, together with her daughter and her family, settled in Ma'ale Adumim, a suburb of Jerusalem.

Virtually immediately after coming to Israel, Anna went to the Holocaust Museum, Yad Vashem. In 1993, Anna and Ivan Sanevich were posthumously awarded the title of "Righteous Among the Nations," along with their three eldest children – Tatyana, Darya, and Petro. Later, the same title was also awarded to their youngest daughter, Stefanina. All of them received medals from Yad Vashem, and their names are inscribed on granite plaques in the Avenue of the Righteous at Yad Vashem. The Righteous Among the Nations have the right to live in Israel, and one of the Sanevich children, Petro, used this right and lives with his family in Beersheba. "And this all became possible" – Anna concludes her memories – "only after I returned, after I entered the city where I had aspired to live my whole life. My city. His city. Jerusalem."

The Lord builds up Jerusalem;
He gathers together the outcasts of Israel.
He heals the brokenhearted
And binds up their wounds.
He counts the number of the stars;
He calls them all by name.
Great is our Lord, and mighty in power;
His understanding is infinite.

Epilogue

And Enoch walked with God;
and he was not,
for God took him.
(Genesis 5:24)

To my great sorrow, I am finishing these pages only after the conclusion of Anna's earthly life. *And she walked with God; and she was not, for God took her.* I think that these words, so significant to her from her very childhood, can be used not only as an epigraph for the Epilogue, not only for this whole book, but also for all of Anna's life: Her life perfectly embodied the great mystery of such an earthly walk before God that later enables one to abide eternally with Him.

Of course, Anna dreamed much about being able to see this book, and I know that from now on, until the end of my earthly journey, this unfulfilled debt to her will leave an open wound in my heart. The story of this book began many years ago when Anna, in response to someone's suggestion to write a book about the incredible story of her and her brother's salvation, unexpectedly for herself, even, resolutely said: Julia Blum will write it. By that time, I had already known and loved Anna for many years, and I had already been writing for many years, but the idea to write about her did not immediately spring to my head; so when Anna called to "inform" me that I would be writing a book about her, I was surprised, to say the least. Naturally, I did not refuse, so as not to upset a person so dear to me and rather elderly; but it was perfectly clear to me that the genre of documental memoires was fundamentally very different from what I had been called to by the Lord and very different from the books based on the Bible and on revelations that He has given me. I put down the receiver with a mixed feeling of concern: I had agreed to something that I shouldn't have, and I hoped: Anna is elderly; over time she would forget, and everything would somehow go away.

It didn't go away. Time passed; I finished my second book – about God's tears over the suffering of Israel – and I began to sense ever more clearly that I should not avoid this new book about Anna, that in some incomprehensible way, this book was also God's plan. Finally, I realized it to the point of meeting with Anna and officially announcing the start of the work. At that very first meeting, the Lord very clearly spoke to my heart about Isaac, giving me the name of the book and confirming more positively than ever before that this was His will and His plan.

And nevertheless, the work advanced very slowly. More than once, I began to doubt: Is this really His will and His plan for me? Writing, rewriting, and restoring Anna's remembrances (and later those of Dmitry, her brother), I always felt that even if I was fulfilling His will and doing His plan, I was missing His revelation. I felt that I could not – and did not want – to write a book in which only man's voice is heard, even if that voice was very precious to me. I wanted to hear from Him; I wanted His voice to fill these pages. But I could not imagine how to realistically go about it, when the pages were already filled with human memories. Yes, the story of their salvation is a wonderful story, and it was unquestionably worthy of being written into a book.
Nevertheless, I still knew that I needed some sort of special goal, some special word that He wanted to speak through this story; otherwise, He would not have assigned it or entrusted me with it. And, trusting in that, I continued to work on the remembrances and awaited His revelations.

My readers know that in recent years, I have written about the mystery that the Lord revealed to me in response to my tears and questioning about the sufferings of Israel: about the mystery of God's special relationship to Israel, about the special place that Israel holds in His heart and in His plan, and about God's vast, though frequently invisible love for Israel, despite all the visible suffering and apparent rejection of our people.

But the time came when I felt that He wanted to open before me some sort of new layers in Israel's relationship with their God. Some time ago, I received the revelation about Isaiah Chapter 29, about the sealed and unsealed Book, but at the time, I did not yet know that it would have a direct correlation to the story of Buzya and Fishl. It took one more revelation from God for it suddenly to become clear to me that the testimony of the brother and sister was the story of the unsealed Book and the Messiah who reveals Himself to His children – a Messiah Who, upon entering their lives, changed everything about their life, yet didn't change anything in the text of this Book itself. Coming to this sudden realization, I once again threw myself into rereading Anna's (Buzya's) recollections and, in flipping through the pages that describe the first 16 years of her life, before she came to believe in Yeshua, I saw for the first time very clearly (as always happens when He Himself shows us something) this smooth, almost imperceptible transition from Buzya's prayers and petitions to God in the ghetto to the acceptance of Yeshua as the Messiah of Israel. Buzya from the ghetto does not yet know Yeshua, and nevertheless, as we see from her prayers, the God of Israel is completely alive and real for her – in some sense, even more true and real than the horror that surrounds her. And when Buzya later hears about Yeshua at the Saneviches, by her own acknowledgement, He is revealed to her not as the God of the gentiles, but as the Messiah of Israel – that same Messiah, whom her family had so waited for and who did not cancel or change, but only strengthened her faith in the God of Abraham, Isaac, and Jacob.

Surprisingly, right during these days as I am finishing this small book, a new, utterly excellent novel by Lyudmila Ulitska came into my possession: *Daniel Stein, Translator.* The book contains many characters, but centers around a Catholic priest named Daniel Stein – a Jew who came to faith in Jesus during the Holocaust. The book describes the story of an actual person, Daniel Rufeisen – a Polish Jew who became a Catholic priest during the Holocaust and lived for much of his life in Israel. It's an excellent book, and I highly recommend it to everyone, but it is incredibly significant to me that the Lord, for Whom there are no coincidences, sent it my way right now when my work on the testimonies of Anna and Dmitry was being written and completed. So, I want to finish my small book by returning to what I already wrote, and what was confirmed once again in Ulitska's book. It was not by meeting with Christian rescuers, no matter how full of light and love they were, but by meeting with **the One Who Himself is Light and Love and Who is revealed on the pages of the unsealed Book before them** that forever changed the life of both Daniel Rufeisen, and Buzya and Fishl Schmieger, along with all those Jews who were themselves *as if slain,* who came out of the fiery suffering of the Holocaust, or other fiery suffering, believing in *the Lamb as if slain.* I think that for the Lord who sat me down over this testimony, specifically this mystery – the mystery of the sealed and unsealed Book – is the most important aspect of the story. This is His word and message that He entrusted me with. *Most assuredly, I say to you, the hour is coming, and now is,*[72] when He Himself, with His hand, will remove the seals of this Book – and then, before the amazed gaze of the *literate* will appear – **will be revealed** – the One Who they least of all expect to see there, Who they thought they knew for certain couldn't, shouldn't be there, **but Who, in fact, had been in the Book from the very beginning.**

Notes:

1. Song of Solomon 8:5

2. Psalms 23:4

3. Isaiah 53:7

4. Matthew 27:40, American King James Version

5. Psalms 79:11

6. Psalms 69:32

7. Romans 8:38-39, Christ Jesus changed to Messiah Yeshua

8. Genesis 5:24

9. Two weeks before the Babi Yar tragedy, on 13 September 1941, in the Peschanoye district, Hitler's supporters shot approximately 3,500 people, mainly women and children. Only a handful of people survived the mass shooting.

10. A socialist hymn

11. Communist Youth League

12. Numbers 23:9

13. Isaiah 55:10-11

14. Psalm 55:12-13

15. Psalm 23: 1-4, emphasis added

16. Ecclesiastes 11:1

17. Matthew 13:8

18. Genesis 22:10

19. Isaiah 29: 11-12

20. Revelation 5:1-4

21. Daniel 12:4

22. Revelation 5:5

23. Isaiah 55:9

24. Zachariah 11:4-5 (NASB)

25. John 5:19

26. Matthew 28:18

27. Zachariah 11:7 (KJV)

28. 2 Corinthians 12:9

29. Psalms 97:5

30. Psalms 18:16-18

31. Hebrews 11:1

32. Acts 8:26-27

33. Jeremiah 32:19

34. Luke 9:24

35. John 12:24

36. Zachariah 11:4

37. John 13:20

38. Matthew 25:40

39. Psalms 40:1-2

40. Mark 1:15

41. 1 John 4:8

42. Hebrews 11:27

43. Revelation 5:5

44. Revelation 5:6

45. Genesis 49:9

46. Matthew 16:17

47. Zachariah 2:9, 2:11, 4:9

48. Psalms 10:15

49. Isaiah 53:3

50. Matthew 29:20

51. Isaiah 53:3

52. Exodus 14:8

53. 2 Kings 6:15-17

54. John 20:29

55. Genesis 24:62

56. Genesis 25:11

57. Philippians 4:13, Christ changed to Messiah

58. Philippians 4:7

59. Psalms 27:4

60. Genesis 3:15

61. Genesis 18:18. See also Genesis 12:2

62. Genesis 49:10

63. Jeremiah 31:31-33

64. John 5:39

65. Ephesians 6:7

66. Genesis 39:5

67. Genesis 24:62

68. Genesis 4:10

69. Romans 8:37

70. Psalms 124:1-2

71. Psalms 147:2-5

72. John 5:25

29409925R00073

Made in the USA
Lexington, KY
29 January 2019